MASTER PIANIST

Plate 1
Portrait of Carl Friedberg, 1936

MASTER PIANIST

The Career and Teaching of Carl Friedberg

JULIA SMITH

PHILOSOPHICAL LIBRARY

New York

Printed in the United States of America

50401

TO MY MOTHER—JULIA MILLER SMITH

FOREWORD

By Dame Myra Hess

To all who knew Carl Friedberg his name will stand for always as a symbol of a great musician—one of the last outstanding personalities of the pre-1914 world where music was an integral and indispensable element of everyday life in Europe. This background colored his whole approach to music and therefore to life. In it he lost all thought of self in his crusade to bring more and ever more music into people's lives, not as a means to fame or profit, but as a source of joy. It was, to him, the natural expression of the spirit and the road to growth and development.

Although I did not meet Carl Friedberg until 1922, when I first went to America under the management of his sister Annie Friedberg, I had long felt the influence of his personality. His name was almost a legend in Europe, where we heard fabulous stories about him. Once, for instance, he arrived in Holland too late for a rehearsal and went on to the stage thinking he was going to play the Brahms D minor Concerto; instead of the long *tutti* he suddenly heard the horn solo which opens the Brahms B flat Concerto, and in the space of one measure he reoriented his mind and gave, from the depths of his musicianship, a superlative performance of a work he happened not to have played for many months.

My first indirect link with him was in 1913, when I had gone to Holland for a weekend to hear a performance of the *St. Matthew Passion*. He was suddenly unable to fulfill an engagement with the Hague Orchestra. I had no concert dress with me, but in borrowed clothes I hurried from Amsterdam to The Hague and played the Beethoven 4th Concerto. I missed the Passion music; but to have taken the place of Carl Friedberg, so beloved in Holland, was a privilege and honour which I have never forgotten.

Unhappily, two world wars have deprived us of hearing him often in public. But during my long friendship with him he has played for me countless times, and the influence of these intimate performances will always remain with me.

His close association and friendship with Clara Schumann and Brahms naturally gave him a keen understanding of the music of the romantic period; but his ultimate interpretations were always the outcome of his own genius and profound integrity. His search was always for beauty, or rather beauty through truth; and this was his touchstone throughout music.

His outlook on all forms of art was unusually broad-minded and adventurous. His interest in contemporary music, in particular, was intense, and was surely due to his spirit of eternal youth which was undimmed until the last day of his life. He seemed never to miss the performance of a new work; or, for that matter, any interesting concert that took place in New York, even when he had reached the age of 80 and had been teaching all day.

This unquenchable enthusiasm, together with his deep musicianship, made him one of the great teachers of our time. For him, each of his students was pre-eminently an individual, both musically and personally, and he gave unstintingly of his wisdom to the general development of every one.

It is a tragedy that we have so few of his recordings. In his humility he remained obdurate for many years; but fortunately, when he was 81, he finally relented and we have a few reminders of the unique and ineffable quality of his playing. These records are worthy of study by all who value the timeless beauty of great art.

The memory of this great artist and personality will remain for ever with those of us who loved and revered him for his genius, his humility, his generosity and his consummate musicianship.

London

CONTENTS

ILLUSTRATIONS

ACKNOWLEDGMENTS

For the reading and expert criticism of Carl Friedberg: I am indebted to Dame Myra Hess, Lonny Epstein, and Gerda Friedberg. To Dame Myra I also give grateful thanks for her beautiful and moving *Foreword* and to Gerda Friedberg for her comprehensive *Postscript:* "A Tribute to the Artist." I also wish to thank my aunt, Dr. Ruby Cumby Smith, for the pleasant hours we spent together reading aloud the final version and for her help in editing the manuscript.

Thanks are likewise due Bruce Hungerford for the loan of numerous tapes of his lessons and conversations with Carl Friedberg; also for the loan of Harriette Brower's out-of-print *Piano Mastery* which contains an important chapter on Carl Friedberg's methods of teaching; and for photographs of the artist-teacher Hungerford made in recent years. All have proved of great help in the writing of this book. Gratitude is extended to Mrs. Friedberg, Hans Friedberg, and Lonny Epstein for the loan of photographs collected through the years which highlight the artist's long career.

Thanks are also due the Friedberg Management, César Searchinger, Director, for the loan of several scrapbooks which contain biographical and professional data relating to Carl Friedberg's career from 1912-1955; the New York Public Library (Forty-second Street Branch) for access to and use of the Carl Friedberg clipping file and other materials; and Mrs. Friedberg for several books of clippings and other documents, all of which have proved most useful in the preparation of the manuscript.

I must also express my indebtedness to Thomas T.

Watkins, Librarian, Columbia University Music Department (where the Carl Friedberg Memorial Library is now permanently placed) for access to certain piano scores from the Friedberg collection.

I further gratefully acknowledge the help of Mrs. Friedberg and of Carl Friedberg's sons, Hans and Curt, in providing me with biographical data not obtainable elsewhere; and the loan by Lonny Epstein and Malcolm Frager of excerpts from certain Friedberg letters, as well as their help in the translation of several critical German writings.

Thanks must be given to Inge Sammet, Carl Friedberg's faithful secretary, for providing the addresses of many of his former pupils and for other essential information. Also recognition is made to my husband, Oscar Vielehr, for his help and encouragement in the preparation of the manuscript.

Moreover, I must acknowledge the help of Marie Liefmann at Frankfurt, a.M., who showed me the Frankfurt of Carl Friedberg's day, including the Clara Schumann house where he visited as a youth, and who provided me with programs saved from the late 1890's and early 1900's. I must likewise mention the assistance given me by Marta Pagels at Cologne, who accompanied me to the site of the Conservatory and the artist's various residences in that city. She too, had kept safely through two terrible wars programs of the Cologne Conservatory Years, newspaper clippings, photographs and the interesting book by Walter Niemann, *Meister des Claviers,* from which an excerpt appears in Chapter IV.

Thanks are also due Sergius Kagen for his revealing article, "The Teaching of Carl Friedberg" which he wrote expressly for this book and which appears at the end of Chapter V; and Grace Castagnetta for her recollections of conversations she enjoyed with Carl Friedberg on a subject dear to his heart, improvization.

Two articles are reproduced by permission of the following owners:
Harriette Brower's chapter "Carl Friedberg" from her book

Piano Mastery (Second Series), copyright 1916 by Oliver Ditson Company, used by permission of the Theodore Presser Company.

Carl Friedberg's article, "Be Prepared" (as told to Rafael Kammerer) which appeared in the January 15, 1954 issue of *Musical America*. Permission given by the Musical America Company.

Finally, acknowledgments are made to the following devoted pupils of Carl Friedberg whose contributions of material have formed the basis for Chapter VII, "Glimpses into the Teaching of Carl Friedberg": Lillian Ball, Helen Brainard, Catherine Carver Burton, Rosalie Briskin Cameron, John Chagy, Betty June Cooper, Robert Darnell, Lonny Epstein, Malcolm Frager, Walter Golz, Ilse Fromm-Michaels, Hans Friedberg, Rosy Geiger-Kullman, Cläre Hanisch, Barbara Holmquest Gotz, Northera Barton Hubbell, Leonard Hungerford, Marie Liefmann, Gwendolyn Marsh, William Masselos, Marienka Michna, Franz Mittler, Sylvia Muehling, Martha Hutcheson Norton, Marta Pagels, Emma Badia de Roca, Vivian Scott, Mary Stretch, Richard Thenebe, Helen Thomson Thomas, Elizabeth Turner, and Lois Whiteman.

Julia Smith

New York City

MASTER PIANIST

BACKGROUND AND EARLY STUDY

Bingen-am-Rhein   Frankfurt-am-Main

(1872-1892)

When Carl Friedberg was announced as soloist for the 1916-1917 Cincinnati Symphony Concert Series during his third American tour, the music editor of the local *Times Star* commented that the noted German pianist ". . . is now in a position to repeat with some reason, should he desire to do so, those lines of the old-fashioned ballad which are associated with the city of his birth:

> *Take a letter and a message*
> *To some distant friends of mine,*
> *For I was born at Bingen,*
> *At Bingen on the Rhine."* [1]

Bingen, near Mainz, a town over 600 years old, noted for its wines, has changed but little through the centuries. Topped by the craggy Scharlachberg, well-cultivated vineyards extend down the mountain slope to the town below where interesting old houses, winding streets and soaring church spires combine to form beautiful and romantic vistas along the Rhine. Bingen, too, has its old medieval castle, the Burg Klopp, located higher up the mountain, which maintains a clear view of the surrounding countryside.

Directly opposite the town on an island in the Rhine is the Mäuseturm (Mouse Tower), close by the Ehrenfels ruin. Just below and downstream, the river winds sharply to the right, leading on to the Lorelei Rock with its famous echo. It is characteristic of this picturesque region, traditionally devoted to the spirit of good fellowship, that the inter-mingling of tender and often sentimental German songs with the still, delicate flavor of the Rhenish wines, has produced a people not only gregarious, romantic and optimistic, but also spontaneous and jocular.

While not positively known, it is generally believed that the Friedberg family came from Prague, Czechoslovakia to Bingen about 1300. During contemporary times members of the family of Carl's mother, for generations prominent as bankers in the small Rhineland city, recall the existence of Friedberg family graves in Bingen dating back to the Fifteenth Century. Although there had been a strong Jewish strain on both sides of the family, later generations have become so intermingled that they are virtually indistinguishable from the familiar local Germanic blonde type.

Carl Rudolph Hermann Friedberg, third child and only son of Eduard and Elise Friedberg (née Landau), was born at Bingen-am-Rhein, Germany, on September 18, 1872. Fair-haired, fair-skinned, blue-eyed, with a delicate constitution and hyper-sensitive nature, young Carl gave evidence at an early age of becoming a musician. His three sisters, at least two of whom were musical, were Henrietta, Annie (the future concert manager) and Mathilde.

Carl's grandfather, Rafael Friedberg, was a wealthy vine-yard-owner whose special interest was painting. One wing of his spacious abode housed a fine collection of paintings, both "old masters" and contemporary works. On one wall hung a portrait of an early Friedberg ancestor, painted by a descendant. Among the friends who came to drink his excellent wines, the grandfather numbered Düsseldorf artists,

2

as well as local musicians, poets and philosophers. Both Carl's father and grandfather were amateur musicians in the traditional German sense.*

Eduard Friedberg, the son, occupied a small house on his father's estate and assisted in the management of the vineyards. When the grapes were ripe the grandchildren might eat all they liked. Almost as soon as Baby Carl could walk and talk he found the way to his grandfather's big house where he was a great favorite. The old man and the young boy shared a deep affection coupled with rare understanding, a relationship the great pianist later recalled with nostalgia. On his grandfather's knee Carl heard from him— or perhaps from some of his artistic friends—the fantastic fairy tales recorded by the Brothers Grimm, the heroic legends of the Nibelungen, the *Tyl Eulenspiegel* drolleries and other Germanic, Central European folklore. At an early age Carl's sensitivity to beauty was so pronounced that he recoiled from the sight of deformity, or ugliness of any kind. This early pursuit of beauty in all its various manifestations became the ideal of the future artist.

During the first years of his childhood Carl's mother was plagued continually by ill health and frequented spas in search of cures, taking little Carl with her. Proof of the curative value of the waters is that his mother was eventually healed of her ailments and lived until she was 81.

Regarded as a prodigy, Carl received his first music lessons at the age of four from Herr Louverse, a Dutch musician and the local Bingen organist. At an early age he played for Anton Rubinstein, who pronounced him a child of great talent. At that time the boy accompanied by his mother attended a piano recital (perhaps by Rubinstein) which greatly impressed him. On returning home and pre-

---

* About 1932, Carl Friedberg showed the writer a small German book, then long out of print, which told of a Viennese court musician, during the time of Haydn, by the name of Friedberg who, he believed, "might have been an early ancestor."

paring for bed, with tearful emotion he said: "I, too, should like to play the piano so beautifully!"

Because of Carl's precocity his father engaged a tutor to begin his formal education. Somewhat later the child attended the local public school where he had as classmate the young Stefan George, now numbered among the great German poets.

Like all boys, Carl was interested in trains and was said to have known by sight and name every engine in the vicinity. In later life he complained that he never played enough with trains. He often said: "If only I had a house where I could have a room big enough for trains."

But from the beginning there was no doubt that music was his calling. Besides studying piano with Herr Louverse, Carl also studied harmony and counterpoint, as the *Contrapunkt* notebook with CARL FRIEDBERG neatly lettered and the address "Bingen a. Rhein" stamped on the cover reveal. Inside, each page is meticulously numbered and each exercise is carefully written in ink. The first forty pages are filled with exercises based on various *Canti Firmi* and old chorale themes, to which Carl wrote strict counterpoint in two, three and four parts. Beginning with the tenth exercise which he has marked "Aufgabe No. 5 von Hiller" and continuing, there are at least thirty such assignments, indicating that he used as text Ferdinand Hiller's *Übungen zum Studium der Harmonie und des Contrapuncts.* (Hiller was then director of the Cologne Conservatory where Carl Friedberg was eventually to teach.) By his eleventh year the boy had progressed as far as two-voice double counterpoint, his exercises revealing a clearly defined melodic sense combined with interesting uses of rhythm.

Following his grandfather's death, Eduard Friedberg took over management of the lucrative vineyards. Having also inherited a considerable fortune, he soon retired from business, in order to devote himself to his family and to leisurely pursuits.

4

According to Annie Friedberg, the second sister, when Carl was about eleven, Herr Louverse suggested to Eduard further study for the boy in a larger town, readily acknowledging that he had taught his talented pupil all that he knew. Often the teacher sensed that the boy anticipated what he would be told.

His father, believing that great talent is often accompanied by the ability to choose the right step ahead, thereupon asked his son: "With whom do you wish to study?" "With Clara Schumann," came the prompt reply.

Mme. Schumann, widely acclaimed as one of the great musicians of the Nineteenth Century, was now quite old. In order for the boy to acquire a firm technical foundation and gain the greatest benefit from her teaching, Louverse advised the father first to place Carl with James Kwast, noted Dutch pianist and teacher who, like Mme. Schumann, was a member of the faculty of the recently-founded Frankfurt Hoch'sche Conservatorium.

For a time the boy, accompanied by his father or mother, travelled fortnightly to Frankfurt-am-Main for piano lessons with Kwast. He made such rapid progress in his studies that his father decided to move the entire family to Frankfurt. There he purchased a pleasant summer-house with a large beautiful garden for the children, located in the West End, on the outskirts of the city. In winter the family lived in an apartment at Ulmenstrasse 49, nearer the center of town.

Frankfurtians of that day recall that Elise Friedberg, Carl's mother (a particularly Scotch-like type, tall of stature, with blue eyes, dark hair, and fine features) was both a famed beauty and a devoted mother.

Frankfurt in the 1880's, at the time the Friedbergs moved there, was a well-known, wealthy and elegant town. In the center was the "old city" with narrow, picturesque streets and quaint houses. Here were the *Römer,* the old town hall, and the cathedral, called the *Dom,* both buildings from the Fifteenth to the Eighteenth Centuries closely connected with the election and coronation of the Emperors of Germany. In this section also stands the restored Goethe House.

The location of Frankfurt in the fertile valley of the Main invited excursions to the *Taunus* mountains on the north, to the *Odenwald* in the south and to the Rhine valley on the west. More easily accessible was the *Stadtwald*, where families went for their afternoon coffee or for supper.

Frankfurt also offered interesting museums and excellent libraries. Besides the Rothschilds, the rich banker family which had its origin in the Frankfurt ghetto, there were many other wealthy families, both Gentile and Jewish, who maintained a keen interest in public welfare, science, the arts and music, and who donated their riches for social, educational and artistic pursuits.

Frankfurt enjoyed a very intensive musical life. The Opera House, (now roofless, its interior gutted by Allied bombings in World War II), the staircase of which resembled that of the Paris Opera presented performances virtually the year round. In the *Museumsgesellschaft*, home of the concert society, were heard orchestral concerts as well as famous instrumental and vocal soloists: pianists, Clara Schumann, Johannes Brahms, Eugen d'Albert, Teresa Carreño; violinists, Joseph Joachim and Pablo de Sarasate; singers; Julius Stockhausen and Ludwig Wüllner.

As in nearly every other town in Germany there were numerous choral societies in Frankfurt, the most important being the *Cäcilien Verein* and the *Rühl'sche Gesangverein*, both mixed choirs, which performed oratorios.

The Hoch'sche Conservatorium, occupies an historic place in musical education, from the first attracting students from all over the world. It was founded in 1877 by Dr. Joseph Paul Johann Hoch, a physician and prominent citizen of Frankfurt, who endowed it with his entire fortune of more than one million marks. Located near the center of the city close by the Eschenheimerturm, the Hoch Conservatory was a handsome stone mansion, three stories high especially constructed for its musical needs.

It is interesting to note that recitals in the modern sense began only in the 1830's with Liszt, Thalberg and Clara Wieck Schumann. Before that a solo recital on the piano, or the public performance of a piano sonata was a rarity. Clara Schumann was acknowledged the greatest living interpreter not only of the music of her husband, but also a sensitive and eloquent interpreter of Johannes Brahms.*

It was Brahms who, in 1877, sensing Clara Schumann's advancing age and the beginning of her physical decline, urged her to accept the post as principal teacher of the pianoforte at the Hoch Conservatory, even though she had a strong dislike for Joachim Raff, its first director.

Accompanied by her daughters Marie and Eugenie, she took residence in Frankfurt in May, 1878, to be there in readiness for the opening of the fall term. The large, comfortable, white stone house, with its open porch and charming garden in the rear, located at 32 Myliusstrasse, remained her permanent home, and here Brahms had his own room when he came to visit. In this house, which still stands, young Carl Friedberg met Johannes Brahms.

On September 25, 1878, the Hoch'sche Conservatorium with 123 pupils was formally opened by the Burgomaster of the ancient free town, Herr von Mumm, on which occasion the director, Joachim Raff, delivered an appropriate address. In addition to Clara Schumann, designated as "Professor of the Higher Pianoforte Classes," the original faculty included Julius Stockhausen, head of the vocal classes; Hugo Heermann, teacher of violin and ensemble playing; Bernhard Cossman and Valentin Müller, teachers of cello; and Franz Magnus, teacher of music history and theory.

* Mme. Schumann played Brahms's solo piano works with the exception of the two piano concerti, finding both beyond her physical powers. She did, however, on one occasion, attempt the D minor.

7

On Brahms's suggestion that Czerny's *Course of Piano Studies,* originally published by Diabelli in Vienna might prove of use to her students at the Hoch Conservatory, Clara Schumann, in 1880, read the *Course* and found much of it excellent. However, she noted that the exercises would be more useful to her pupils in a selected edition. Upon inquiry to August Cranz, music publisher in Hamburg, as to whether he had brought out a selection of the studies, he answered that he had not, but would be very much pleased if Mme. Schumann would herself undertake such an edition. She agreed, and work was at once started.[2] When completed it was published by Cranz under the title of *Exercises and Studies from Carl Czerny's Great School of Pianoforte Playing, Op. 500. Selected and edited by Clara Schumann.** Mme. Schumann was of the opinion that the student who mastered these selected Czerny exercises would encounter no technical difficulties in playing Beethoven's sonatas and concertos.

Among artists who made a strong impression on the youthful Carl Friedberg was Hans von Bülow. He appeared with his famous Meiningen Orchestra in a concert at Frankfurt in 1884. The program included the second piano concerto (B flat Major) of Brahms. Von Bülow played the solo part, conducting from his seat at the piano, and both pianist and orchestra performed the extended work to perfection. The youth was intrigued by the virtuosic display of talents, and it is quite likely that his own later interest in conducting received an impetus from this performance.

In the absence of records, destroyed with the building in the bombings of World War II, it is believed that Carl Friedberg was a student at the Hoch Conservatory in 1883, or 1884, where he enrolled in the regular piano course with

* This undoubtedly was an incentive to Brahms to publish, in 1891 (Simrock), his 51 *Übungen für das Pianoforte,* studies he had written over a long period of time.

James Kwast, whose pupil he was for four years. He studied theory and composition with Iwan Knorr and Bernhard Scholz, with the latter of whom he also studied score-reading and conducting.*

James Kwast, who must be regarded as Carl Friedberg's principal teacher, was born in Holland in 1852 and was, at the time Carl studied with him, married to the daughter of Ferdinand Hiller, Antonie, or "Toni," as she was familiarly called. Their home in Frankfurt was the meeting-place for various celebrities passing through the city. Brahms, Rubinstein, Clara Schumann and Julius Stockhausen were among their intimate friends. It was in the Kwast home that the youth met many of the traveling virtuosi and famous composers, for many of whom he played at the insistence of his proud teacher.

In addition to Carl Friedberg, the list of students at the Hoch Conservatory during these early years, to mention only a few, included the American, Edward MacDowell, who as a youth of 18 from 1879-1882 studied composition with Raff; the Englishman, Cyril Scott, who studied piano with James Kwast in 1891, and returned to Frankfurt in 1895, to study composition with Iwan Knorr; the Australian, Percy Grainger, Hans Pfitzner and, later, Otto Klemperer, all three of whom were pupils of Kwast; Ernest Bloch, who studied composition with Knorr in 1900; many of Mme. Schumann's pupils, including Mathilde Verne, Adelina de Lara and three English pianists, Fanny Davies, Amina Goodwin and Leonard Borwick; Walther Lampe, a pupil of Knorr and Humperdinck; Max Alvary and Johannes Messchaert, pupils of Stockhausen.

While attending the Hoch Conservatory Carl also pursued his general education at the gymnasium, the equivalent of an American high school, where he proved himself a superior student in all subjects, showing especial aptitude

* Following Raff's death in 1882, Scholz suceeded him as director of the Hoch Conservatory.

in mathematics. He completed the requirements for graduation from the *gymnasium* at fifteen, an unprecedented age, for eighteen was the average. In order for the lad to accept this earned graduation honor at so early an age, his parents necessarily requested and received permission from the government.

The possessor of creative as well as interpretative gifts, Carl also, at fifteen, had written and conducted his first "Sinfonietta," which work was performed with great success at the Hoch Conservatory in one of the student composition concerts.

Turning again to Carl's *Contrapunkt* notebook, we see that Professor Knorr, the boy's composition teacher, prominent also as a composer, did not base his teaching on textbook assignments. We learn that he had progressed to the study of fugue, for many pages are filled with fugue subjects followed by "real" and "tonal" answers. Later on, appear sketches of two- and three-voice fugues and of "free" compositions, such as an entry of five bars scored for string quartet to which he has given the title "Humoresque"; also an outline for a four-voice vocal composition with organ accompaniment; and finally a short orchestral excerpt in full score, which may have been a fragment of his "Sinfonietta" written about this time.

Other of his childhood musical inspirations are a "Fugue on a Theme of Haydn," a "Böhmisches Volkslied" for string quartet, with the upper voices written in the tonality of E minor and the lower in E Major. There also appear sketches of a *Charakterstücke für das Pianoforte, betitelt die vier Jahreszeiten* with the subtitles: "Frühling, Sommer, Herbst, Winter"; and a suite for string quartet with short pieces entitled: "Marsch, Andante con Variazoni, Scherzo, Zigeunertanz, Fugue."

These happy, carefree days of Carl Friedberg's early youth were spent in the pursuit of both mental and artistic

10

development with the lad's absorbing, like a thirsty sponge, everything with which he came in contact—reading Goethe, Schiller and Heine, spending long hours at the art museums and library, besides his studies at the *gymnasium* and his piano lessons.

For relaxation the boy preferred long, lonely walks in the dark, silent woods. As is often the case with persons of multiple talents, Nature's sounds inspired him musically, most of all, the songs of birds. The polarity of youth and age were strongly marked in him. As a youth he seemed old for his age, and mature. Conversely, in his old age, he appeared buoyant and youthful.

So far as we know, Carl studied with Mme. Schumann for only one or two years, but played for her intermittently thereafter as her health permitted. From James Kwast he acquired a serviceable and dependable technique. His contact with Mme. Schumann, though brief, resulted in the acquisition of her particular approach to the music of Robert Schumann, Brahms and other composers plus the implication of her total artistic personality, her unique *Kultur*. And of what did Mme. Schumann's artistic personality consist?

As an artist, Clara Schumann was thought by many to rank higher than any of her contemporaries; perhaps not so much in the degree of her natural and cultivated gifts as in the uses she made of them. Franklin Taylor, who studied with her, has said that Mme. Schumann's playing was characterized by an "entire absence of personal display, a keen perception of the composer's meaning, and an unfailing power of setting it forth in perfectly intelligible form." She was famous for the beautiful quality of her tone production, which was vigorous and full without sounding harsh. This she obtained, even in fortissimo passages, "by pressure with the fingers rather than by percussion. Indeed," continues Taylor, "her playing was particularly free from violent movement of any kind: in passages, the fingers were kept close to the keys and squeezed [pressed] instead of striking them, while chords were grasped from the wrist rather than struck from the elbow." Her technique was founded on the principle advanced by her father-teacher, Friedrich Wieck, that "the touch [i.e., the blow of the finger upon the key] should never be audible, but only the musical sound." [3]

Her repertory was large, extending from Scarlatti and Bach to Mendelssohn, Chopin, Robert Schumann and Brahms, all of which she performed admirably; and it must be noted, to Mme. Schumann's everlasting credit, that she not only was herself a composer, but that she also was interested in the music of her contemporaries as well as in the music of the great masters. Her interest in the music of certain of the composers of her day was one of the important aspects of her teaching, which she transmitted to her pupils and which Carl Friedberg, in turn, was faithfully to transmit to his own pupils.

While little is known of his actual lessons with Clara Schumann other than the fact that he played for her virtually all the piano works of Mozart, Beethoven, Mendelssohn, Chopin, Liszt and Robert Schumann, Dr. Gerhard Tischer, an early champion of Friedberg's dynamic pianism, has commented that "his soft touch is probably due to her influence." [4]

To one of his American pupils Friedberg later spoke of his first visit to the great musician. "I was fifteen when I went to see Clara Schumann, who at that time [1887] must have been about 68 years old. She wore a little lace cap like the ones you see in her pictures, and long, full, black silk skirts. After she sat down, consuming several minutes to adjust her skirts carefully, she looked at me and asked: 'What will you play?' I knew all the works of Robert Schumann from memory at that time and so played the G

12

Plate 2
Clara Schumann towards the end of her life

Plate 3
Brahms in his latter years

minor *Sonata, Papillons* and several of the *Scenes from Childhood*. She said: 'You like my husband's music?' I replied: 'Yes,' full of respect. After I had played a number of works by other composers, including some little pieces of my own, she said simply: 'You are talented. I will accept you as a pupil.' "

Later, at lessons, Mme. Schumann criticised Carl's playing very little, sensing that the boy's inborn musicianship would lead him to a natural understanding in the interpretation of the music.

An illustration of this is revealed in recollections of a lesson on the Schumann piano concerto, as told by Friedberg to one of his younger "last pupils." Clara Schumann had prepared a very careful edition of Robert Schumann's music, marking explicitly the tiniest details, insisting that her pupils carry them out to the letter. However, the youthful Carl had the boldness to suggest that a staccato passage following the lyrical theme of the last movement (approximately sixteen measures) which she had indicated to be played with short touches of the pedal would, in reality, sound much clearer without any pedal at all. He played it for her both ways and Mme. Schumann agreed with him that the particular passage in question "really sounds better without *any* pedal."

Brahms, then about 54, came frequently from Vienna to visit her, often bringing along with him his newest compositions which he was eager to have Clara Schumann hear and criticize before they were presented to the general public. It was to her that he first brought his cello *Sonata Op.* 99, his violin *Sonata Op.* 100, and his *Trio in C minor Op.* 101, for which works he had as assisting players the violinist Joseph Joachim (also a devoted friend of both Clara and Brahms) and the cellist, Robert Hausmann. This was possibly in the fall of 1886, for Brahms had written these three works during the previous summer; more probably it was the fall of 1887 since Brahms's postcard to

13

Clara, dated simply "September 1887," requested a rehearsal of these works in her house on September 18.[5]

Because Clara Schumann did not see very well, she asked young Carl, who had been invited to be present at the rehearsal and who even then was an avid admirer of Brahms's music, to turn pages for him. (Carl had previously seen the great composer only once before when he had heard Brahms conduct his Fourth Symphony at the Frankfurt Museum concerts in November, 1885.) Remembering this thrilling moment at Mme. Schumann's house in later years, Friedberg recalled that he was delighted to be asked to render this service to his idol and, almost breathless with excitement at the honor, asked him once throughout the entire rehearsal: "Am I turning the pages all right? 'Very good,' Brahms said, his beard wobbling. And then, after the C minor *Trio* was finished, a servant brought in a tray of glasses, beer and cognac which she served. I was sitting still on Brahms's left side. He turned around and said: 'Do you like that music?' I said: 'If it is not too immodest, I might say, I love it!' 'You understand it?' he asked. 'I don't know—I only know that I love it!' I replied. 'Of these three works, which do you like best?' he asked. I said: 'They can't be compared with each other, they are so different. I like especially, if I may say so, the conciseness and penetrating shortness of form in the C minor *Trio*.' Brahms was very pleased at my answer. 'You have studied form? Can you compose?' he asked. 'A little bit,' I said. 'Now,' said Brahms, 'the first movement of the *Trio* I have constructed according to the C minor *Symphony*. That is why it is so good in form,' he revealed." And Carl Friedberg, after more than sixty years' intimate knowledge of this music, still regarded this movement as "one of the marvelous sonata forms."

The youthful musician heard Brahms play a total of eight times. He again turned pages for his hero when Brahms played with Clara Schumann the Robert Schumann *Varia-*

tions and his own *Variations on a Theme of Haydn.** (It may have been this very occasion that inspired Carl to write the charming set of "Variations über ein Tema von Robert Schumann in E moll" ** for string quartet, the manuscript being dated "Frankfurt, 14. Mai 1889," when he was seventeen years old. Based on No. 16, "Erster Verlust" [First Loss] from the *Album für die Jugend Op.* 68, Carl has presented the theme with eight variations, the finale a fugue, all very much in the style of Robert Schumann.)

"I was always a good page-turner," continued Friedberg, speaking to one of his pupils in later years, "and I turned pages for him when he played the G minor Piano Quartet and he was half drunk. Never were the two hands together. His tempi, though, were very good."

On October 20, 1888, Clara Schumann celebrated in Frankfurt and also in Leipzig her artistic Diamond Jubilee, the 60th Anniversary of public appearances. On this occasion she performed with great acclaim the Mozart D minor *Concerto,* playing, as she often did, her own cadenzas. Carl Friedberg spoke of this performance many years later to some of his American pupils as one of his most beautiful and vivid musical memories of Mme. Schumann.

Among other recollections of his teacher was the expressive playing of her husband's *Concerto in A Minor* with the Frankfurt Museums Orchestra when Carl again acted as page-turner. On another occasion at the Hoch Conservatory when the youth performed particularly well a Beethoven *Sonata* he had been studying, a mutual friend recalls that Mme. Schumann bestowed a kiss of approbation upon her gifted pupil.

By the winter of 1888, the Friedberg family found itself

---

* Mme. Schumann and Brahms were then editing the complete works of Robert Schumann for Breitkopf und Haertel later published as the "Clara Schumann Edition."

** Found among Carl Friedberg's student manuscripts.

in straitened circumstances and the boy could no longer devote all his time to the study of music, for it became necessary for him to earn money in order to help support the family.

When circumstances looked their gloomiest, aid came from a most unexpected source. A young lady with a class of some eighteen private piano pupils was soon to be married to a gentleman, resident of another city. Looking about for someone to take over her class, a friend suggested young Carl, who was already recognized as a talented pianist. On her approach to him the youth immediately accepted and this was the beginning of his piano teaching.

At about this time Julius Stockhausen, the great singing-teacher, who numbered among his pupils some of the best-known European singers of that day, was in need of a studio-accompanist and coach. Having observed that Carl was an excellent ensemble player, who read easily at sight even the most difficult music, including orchestral scores, and who transposed readily into all keys, Stockhausen offered him the position, which was eagerly accepted. Thus, while still in his formative years, Carl had the good fortune to work not only with Stockhausen, but also with such other artists as Anton Sistermanns, close friend of Clara Schumann, who first introduced the Schumann *Lieder* to the public; Anton Van Rooy and Jacques Urlus, both Dutch tenors who later sang Wagnerian roles at the Metropolitan Opera; Maria Phillippi, the Swiss soprano, and Nordewyr Redingius, both famous oratorio singers, accompanying on concert tours these and many others.

Just as he phrased, or breathed at the same moment and place in the music with the singer in order to achieve per-fection in ensemble, mood and expressivity, even so Carl learned to prepare every phrase of his piano solo works with the same inhalation, often humming to himself to carry the phrase-line naturally. From this early date the "singing approach" to instrumental music, which was to become one of the prime characteristics of Carl Friedberg's interpretative style, became his ideal. It was from Stockhausen that the youth first heard mention of Hugo Wolf and his new modern *Lieder*.

At seventeen Carl became entirely self-supporting. In addition to teaching and accompanying, he maintained himself by copying music and conducting some of the smaller choral groups in the city. Because of his pronounced musical talent he had already become a scholarship pupil at the Hoch Conservatory.

On Stockhausen's recommendation Carl became the permanent pianist for all the *Museumsgesellschaft* concerts, accompanying not only the artists who coached with Stockhausen, but also all the visiting singers and instrumental artists, including the violinists Ysaye, Joachim, Heermann and the cellist, Hugo Becker. Although Ysaye was fourteen years older than young Friedberg and already an established artist, their life-long friendship dated from that time.

Among visiting composers of note at the Museum concerts during those years were Tschaikovsky and Grieg. In 1889, the Russian composer toured the German cities of Berlin, Dresden, Cologne and Frankfurt as conductor of his own works. In the month of February "the little man with the glasses," as Carl remembered him, conducted his third *Suite* and his first piano *Concerto* (B flat minor) with Sapellnikov as soloist, which latter work young Friedberg liked immensely and which he immediately added to his repertory. Tschaikovsky had also rehearsed his 1812 *Overture* for the concert, but the bombastic "Finale" so frightened the local manager that he suggested another work be chosen. Since the composer had no other of his works with him, only the *Suite* and *Concerto* were performed at this concert. Grieg appeared shortly afterward as soloist in his *Concerto in A minor*.

In 1890, Engelbert Humperdinck, former pupil of Hiller and later of Rheinberger and an ardent Wagnerite became a professor at the Hoch Conservatory, as well as music critic for the *Frankfurter Zeitung,* and Carl Friedberg, now a youth of eighteen, became his pupil in orchestration. Humperdinck was in the process of composing his masterpiece, the opera *Hänsel und Gretel,* and Carl assisted his teacher both in writing out some of the pages of the orchestral score and in copying the instrumental parts. He also made for publication the original piano-vocal score (orchestral reduction) to his teacher's fairy-tale opera, a fact not generally known.

Professor Knorr proved himself a false prophet when he said to Humperdinck regarding *Hänsel und Gretel:* "You know, Engelbert, this opera of yours is much too primitive. People won't like it. Why, you won't even be able to get a dog to give up his warm place by the stove to go hear it!"

Two "Examination Concert" programs (Nos. 4 and 5) from the Hoch Conservatory have been preserved: the first dated May 6, 1890, reveals that Carl played the piano part from the "Andante and Finale" of Mendelssohn's *Sonata in B Flat Major for Violoncello and Piano;* the second, a few days later indicates he accompanied a "Clarinet Sonata" composed by Alex Goldschmidt, a pupil from Dr. Scholz's composition class.

Carl's student compositions include a "Rhapsodie," "2 Charakterstücke," "Fugue à 3," "Fugue à 4 (für Orgel)," "Scherzo," "Praeludium und Fugue (F moll)," "Valse brillante," all seriously worked out and characteristically pianistic.*

Gustave Kogel, conductor of the Frankfurt Museums Orchestra from 1891-1903, introduced there the works of the then "modern" school, from Berlioz, Liszt and Wagner to Brahms, Tschaikovsky and Richard Strauss. During Kogel's

* In manuscript, and placed with his *Contrapunkt* notebook.

first season Carl, at the age of nineteen, played the second performance, and the first in Frankfurt, of Richard Strauss's *Burleske,* then in manuscript, which he learned in twenty-four hours when Eugen d'Albert, who played the first performance and to whom the work is dedicated, was unable to appear.*

Shortly afterward, the young pianist made his first tour of Spain as accompanist for the violinist, Sarasate. They appeared in all the important cities and Carl had the opportunity to perform several solos on each program.

The morning following their concert in Madrid, Sarasate presented his younger colleague to the Queen. While she was conversing with the young pianist her son came into the palace drawing-room. After his introduction to young Friedberg he asked immediately: "Can you play something from *Fledermaus?*" Whereupon Carl sat down at the piano and delighted the Royal Family with a medley of tunes, improvised on the spot, from the operetta which was then all the rage in Europe.

Returning home after his tour Carl found that his beloved teacher, Clara Schumann, had fallen into a state of melancholia accompanied by extreme depression. Furthermore, she was always haunted by the sound of music which kept her from resting. Her last public appearance was in November, 1890, when she performed the Chopin F minor *Concerto* at one of the Museum concerts. The following year, because of her declining health, she gave up most of her teaching. In the spring of 1892 she resigned from her post, although continuing to teach a few of her most gifted students at home. There Carl played for her as often as pos-

---

* Although Oscar Thompson credits Friedberg with the first performance of the *Burleske,* in 1898, this is undoubtedly in error, for d'Albert is stated elsewhere to have first performed the work in June, 1890, at the Eisenach Festival. See *International Cyclopedia of Music and Musicians,* p. 630.

sible, for he was on the eve of a momentous concert—a Viennese debut, with orchestra.

Thus it was in the fall of 1892, at the age of twenty, that Carl Friedberg made his debut with the Vienna Philharmonic Orchestra, Gustav Mahler, conducting. This performance immediately established him as an artist to be reckoned with. The critic, Eduard Hanslick, proclaimed him:

A NEW STAR OF THE UTMOST IMPORTANCE!

"We heard a young man from Germany, by the name of Carl Friedberg," Hanslick wrote, "who yesterday played the Bach [D Minor] 'Concerto' and the César Franck 'Variations' in the Philharmonic, and not only did he deserve the distinction 'guest of the Philharmonic' * but he adorned the whole concert with these classical works." [6]

From this moment the young artist's unique career began its steady ascent.

---

* It was rare that a soloist was engaged with this orchestra.

II

THE FRANKFURT CONSERVATORY YEARS

(1893-1904)

Despite his promising Vienna debut Carl Friedberg found concert engagements as a solo pianist few and far between. d'Albert and Busoni were reigning favorites, and it was difficult for a new pianist to attract the attention of concert managers and orchestral conductors. Nevertheless, he managed to secure appearances before several European royal persons who took a great interest in his talents. Among these was Carmen Sylva, pen-name of Queen Elizabeth of Roumania,* a gifted story-teller and poet, whose writings had become well-known on the continent.

On one occasion when the Roumanian Queen was visiting her mother, Princess of Wied, at the latter's magnificent castle on the Rhine where the aristocrats of art and music often assembled, the Princess invited the young pianist to give a concert. In addition to several classical works, Carl performed for the assembled guests his own recently completed suite of six piano pieces entitled *Stimmungen*** (Moods).[1] Though only twenty, his poetic playing and artis-

---

* Elizabeth was the wife of King Carol I and they were the immediate predecessors of King Ferdinand and Queen Marie.

** Published by Breitkopf und Härtel, 1893, The *Suite* has the following sub-titles: 1) *Wehmütig,* 2) *Ärgerlich,* 3) *Träumerisch,* 4) *Lustig,* 5) *Sehnsuchtsvoll,* 6) *Heftig erregt.*

tic appearance, together with his talented compositions, made a strong impression on the Queen. Subsequently she sent him several of her poems with the wish that he set them to music. One of their musical collaborations, entitled *Ständchen,* was later published by André.[2] Two other songs, "Todesgang" and "Über den Garten, über die Au'," composed about that time, are very likely settings of Carmen Sylva's lyrics.[*] Carl also became a frequent visitor at Neuwied, the residence of the Princess.

Nearer to his heart than composing (to him, merely the setting down of notes) was Carl's greater gift, improvisation, a lost art today but for a few exceptions—notably that of the American pianist, Grace Castagnetta, and the Englishman, Alec Templeton, both of whom Friedberg greatly admired. The tendency to improvise was so strong a part of Carl's nature that it colored his entire approach to life; so much so that it is not inaccurate to say of him that he "improvised" his way through life.

As a youth he often sat for hours at the piano, extemporizing on a theme of his own, or on one from "the Masters," or even, at times, on a folksong. Equipped with a perfect ear, he was able, upon the single hearing of a composition, to reproduce it immediately at the piano, note-perfect. This was demonstrated on one occasion when he heard Anton Rubinstein in a recital at Frankfurt play his "Valse Caprice," still in manuscript. After only the one hearing, Carl in a recital in which he appeared on the following night at the Hoch Conservatory, both delighted and mystified his audience by playing Rubinstein's "Valse Caprice" as an encore!

Meanwhile the young pianist concertized whenever and wherever possible. No distance was too great for him to travel nor was any fee too small to accept as long as it gave the young artist the opportunity to perform. He continued

---

[*] The name of the author of the texts does not appear in the manuscript.

to offer his own works, especially the *Stimmungen** suite, and introduced his new "Gavotte," ** which became popular not only with audiences, but also with other pianists who used it frequently as an encore. Although his youthful works show the influence of Bach, Robert Schumann and Brahms, their "daring" modulations and colorful harmonic language reveal also that Richard Strauss had begun to influence him.

In his struggle for artistic recognition, Carl's ability to accompany proved his most lucrative source of income, and as an accompanist he was generally acknowledged supreme. During the fall of 1892 at Berlin, he accompanied Anton Sistermanns in three *Lieder* recitals, performing songs of Robert Franz, Cornelius, Schubert, Brahms and Schumann. In subsequent seasons he again joined with Sistermanns in presenting Schubert's *Die Schöne Müllerin* and Schumann's *Dichterliebe.****

In 1893 Carl Friedberg was engaged as a teacher at the Frankfurt Conservatory (Hoch'sche Conservatorium) where he taught until 1904.

Among the many artists who visited Frankfurt almost every season and with whom Friedberg became friendly were d'Albert, a former pupil of Liszt whom Hans von Bülow proclaimed the pianistic successor of the aging Rubinstein. d'Albert was married to his second wife, Teresa Carreño, who made an unforgettable impression upon young Friedberg by her playing of Liszt's E major *Polonaise*. Besides this interesting couple, Friedberg knew Paderewski, Rosenthal, Sauer, Busoni, Frederic Lamond, Alexander Siloti and the young Josef Hofmann.

New violinists then were Arrigo Serato and Leopold Auer, with Kreisler, Thibaud, Enesco, Carl Flesch, Huber-

* Dedicated to Constance Schweich, Paris.
** The "Gavotte" was published by Ochler in 1897.
*** One of Friedberg's pupils from that early time wrote that "the spell he wove and the enchantment he cast with his beautiful playing caused the audience to forget the singer."

mann and Elman just beginning their careers; while the older Joachim, Heermann, Sarasate and César Thomson were always in demand as soloists or performers of chamber music.

In 1893 when Carl Friedberg was only 21, the great Brahms Festivals took place. Coincident with the many concerts presented that year was Carl's recital, probably the very first all-Brahms recital ever given, which he played at Bösendorfer Hall in Vienna. The program consisted of the F sharp minor *Sonata,* the two books of the *Paganini Variations,* four pieces from *Op.* 76, four from *Op.* 118, the two *Rhapsodies* and several of the *Waltzes.* Brahms attended, and after the concert, going backstage, he left the hall with the youthful artist who, proud of the great ovation he had received, said to the composer: "The applause, Herr Brahms, was due to *you* . . . not to *me.*"

Years later, recalling this eventful occasion to one of his pupils, Friedberg said: "Brahms took me to the *Tonkünstler Verein,* an association of musicians of which he was the revered Honorary President, who were celebrating the birthday of Ignaz Brüll that night [November 7]. Later in the evening he took me to the Imperial Coffeehouse; (Brahms never wanted to go to bed early), and he said not a single word about my recital until about three o'clock in the morning! Then he simply stroked his beard and said: 'You know you played well—wonderfully, young man! But you must not do that again. You must not play a whole evening of Brahms. People don't like that—I am not popular enough. Play other things, and play only *one* work of mine— you do me a better service.' The humility of such a man!"

Brahms also attended, in November, 1894, a concert in the Frankfurt Museum (Kogel, conductor), to hear a program of his works, including the *Tragic Overture,* the *Violin Concerto* (with Joachim as soloist), *Variations on a Chorale by Haydn* and the *First Symphony.* Clara Schumann was well enough to be present, sitting in the first row with Brahms

24

who was obliged to rise and take many bows. After the concert Friedberg (now a respected young teacher at the Conservatory) and others attended a small gathering in Mme. Schumann's home, honoring the composer and the participating artists.

According to Friedberg, Brahms possessed a physical weakness about which few people knew: he was color-blind. "That has to my mind a certain reflection in his orchestration," commented Friedberg to a pupil many years later. "It is not colorful enough. But he played with so much gusto and freedom. He must have been a wonderful pianist in his younger years! I heard him play the D minor and B flat piano concertos with Nikisch conducting the Gewandhaus Orchestra in 1893. There was another occasion, perhaps at the Berlin Brahms Festival, during the same year, when d'Albert played the concertos and Brahms conducted. He conducted very well—a little bit heavy, however. He had no real technique, what we call now 'modern conductors' technique' like Mitropoulos or Toscanini. Earlier I had also heard him conduct the E minor (Fourth Symphony) with the Frankfurt Museums Orchestra [March 5, 1885]."

Friedberg often visited Brahms in Vienna at his house in the Karlsgasse and not only attended concerts with the master, but also played for him.

After a concert which they attended together Brahms took his younger colleague to his favorite Cafe, Grössenwahn, where they sat until dawn drinking coffee, Brahms smoking one of his long black cigars, and talking of music in general.

At about six A.M. he said to the young man: "Come home with me and I will show you what I mean concerning certain phrasings, tempi, and personal interpretations of my work." And through the early dawn, the two walked to Brahms's house. Here the composer made coffee, opened a bottle of his special cognac, and after they had refreshed themselves, seated himself at the piano and musically clarified his spoken thoughts of the earlier evening hours.

25

During several subsequent visits Brahms played all of his piano compositions for young Friedberg with the exception of the *Paganini Variations*. "His dexterity was not equal to that difficult work anymore," recalled the eminent pianist. "He paused only now and then to pick up a pencil to jot down new and more definitive marks of expression than the published editions indicated. He took pains to explain certain intricacies, to interpret different readings." Friedberg long cherished those precious sheets of music annotated by Brahms's own hand.

On one of these visits Friedberg rehearsed the Beethoven *Sonata Op.* 96, for violin and piano with Joachim, and Brahms turned pages. Beginning with the opening trill in the violin part, Brahms argued with the violinist that *every* Beethoven trill should have an afterbeat as in Brahms's own music, which statement Joachim violently disputed. Decidedly in agreement with the violinist on the manner of playing the Beethoven trills, Friedberg later observed to a pupil that, nevertheless, this particular opening trill is always a matter of dispute between violinists and pianists.

It was in 1895 that the Viennese critic Eduard Hanslick, the most famous and most brilliant musical writer of his day, arch foe of Wagner and staunch champion of Brahms, published his small book, *The Beautiful in Music,* still regarded as a milestone in aesthetics. Through Brahms, young Friedberg knew Hanslick and enjoyed many hours of discussion with them. Friedberg was of the opinion that Hanslick's greatest service to the musical world was in teaching music critics that they should base their writings on aesthetics and not on technic.

Although Brahms was thought to be antagonistic to Wagner, Friedberg did not believe that this was true, as indicated by the latter's account of a performance of the *Siegfried Idyll* in Vienna by the Philharmonic Orchestra (Hans Richter, conductor), at which Brahms was present with him.

"Brahms sat forward in the box, listening intently, never withdrawing his attention for a moment," Friedberg said. "When the concert was over, he got up in silence and, motioning me to follow, strode out. For a long time we walked, with not a word spoken. I, with all the awe of the humblest disciple, never considered breaking the silence, and Brahms said nothing at all, only stomped on, his brows knit, his hat pulled down over them. Finally, a sharp nudge from his powerful elbow almost sent me reeling. We stopped; he stood regarding me with troubled eyes under their shaggy brows.

" 'But you can't hear it every day!' he shouted and stood staring at me, as if wishing me to dispute or agree with him. What I answered I don't now recall, but what stands out vividly is the fact that Brahms was intensely moved by the *Siegfried Idyll,* as I plainly saw, and he was not a man easily stirred, or given to theatrical outbursts either. Whatever his reactions to Wagner's music were, indifference was not among them." [4]

"Brahms was at heart a really kind, tender-hearted person which he tried to cover up by appearing rough," commented Friedberg one day to a pupil. "He behaved in an ill-mannered way at a dinner given for Saint-Saëns on the occasion of one of the French composers visits to Vienna, at which I was present. Following an evening of wining and dining Saint-Saëns was called upon for a speech. With his sparkling Gallic wit he made some references to Beethoven to which Brahms (who had obviously drunk too much) took offense. Rising, he rudely interrupted the speaker, saying: 'How dare you criticize the great composer of a nation that has given you more recognition than your own!' and stalked noisily from the banquet hall, much to the embarrassment of the assembled guests."

At this time Friedberg was at the beginning of his career as a performer of chamber music. To this more intellectual music he transferred easily and naturally his wonderfully sensitive and "spiritual" accompanying gifts—from the vocal instruments with words to the songful instruments without words, bringing to the latter's larger musical form his solo gifts, which were of a high order. The combination of these two imposing qualities of musicianship, rarely found among pianists even today, created a demand for his participation as assisting artist with the leading trio and quartet ensembles of his era.

He first gained fame as the pianist member of sonata teams and, in 1894, appeared in Vienna with the noted cellist, Hugo Becker. There, in Bösendorfer Hall, the two artists presented an all-Beethoven program, which included the two sonatas for piano and cello (C, D,), *Op.* 102. At the Frankfurt Museum's chamber-music concerts between 1894-1900, he performed with Becker the Saint-Saëns piano and cello *Sonata* and the Brahms *Op.* 99, in F Major.

He also performed as the pianist member of the trio comprising Becker and Heermann. This was the first of several noted ensembles to which Friedberg eventually belonged, for he was never satisfied to remain simply a virtuoso. Heermann was the leader of the well-known Frankfurt Museums Quartet and Becker was its cellist. Like himself, both men were also members of the Hoch Conservatory faculty. The other two members of the quartet were Fritz Bassermann, second violinist, and J. Naret-Koning, violinist. With these men Friedberg also presented during that time César Franck's F sharp minor piano *Trio;* two piano quartets, *Op.* 13, by Richard Strauss and *Op.* 60, in C minor, by Brahms; two piano quintets—*Quintet in E minor* by Christian Sinding and *Op.* 4, in F minor by Giovanni Sgambati; and, occasionally, also Beethoven's Triple Concerto in C, *Op.* 56, with orchestra.

Although orchestral performances were still not plenteous for the young artist, nevertheless, at Frankfurt, where he was already highly regarded as a pianist and teacher, Friedberg (now twenty-three) was one of several pianists engaged to appear with that orchestra during the 1895-1896 season, the others being d'Albert, Busoni, and Ernst Pauer.

By virtue of these and similar experiences coupled with his own thirst for knowledge and for truth, Carl Friedberg was developing into a man of remarkable versatility. During the last ten to fifteen years of the Nineteenth Century his superior intellect and active, restless spirit explored many fields, all of which enriched his playing and teaching. At the University of Heidelberg he followed the lectures of Kuno Fischer, becoming thoroughly conversant with the teachings of Socrates, Plato, Aristotle, Rousseau, Hegel and others. He was then most influenced by the writings of Nietzsche, Schopenhauer and Kant, in that order. Nietzsche's *The Case of Wagner* interested him greatly, for though he never came in contact with the great opera composer who died in 1883, he had the opportunity to meet his widow, Cosima, daughter of Liszt and former wife of Hans von Bülow, who occasionally visited in Frankfurt where she had formerly lived.

According to John Erskine, who termed him "a thoroughly original genius," Friedberg was much interested in medicine. His attitude toward himself and, to some extent, toward his pupils was that of a physician.[5] Later in life he became interested in psychoanalysis and followed the writings of both Freud and Jung, attending lectures by Dr. Jung in Switzerland.

Two works given their first Frankfurt performances during the 1895-1896 season that made a strong impression on young Friedberg, were Brahms's *German Requiem* and Bruckner's *Seventh Symphony.*

Humperdinck, critic of the *Frankfurter Zeitung*, cited the latter work as one of the most important events of the musical season. "I cannot understand," he wrote, "why people accuse Bruckner of exaggerating Wagner's principles. The use of four tubas, or daring harmonic connections, is a mere accident, not the essence of Wagner's art. To see that, we must dig deeper, and we must also give to Bruckner that which is Bruckner's, for he is in his way as original as is Brahms, Schumann or Mendelssohn." [6]

In March of the same season Richard Strauss was guest conductor at the Museums concerts, repeating his *Till Eulenspiegels lustige Streiche* (given its world premiere in Frankfurt in September, 1895), and conducting the *Prelude to Act II* of his first opera *Guntram*. Busoni appeared as soloist in the same concert, playing Rubinstein's Fifth Piano Concerto. Friedberg, who was already quite friendly with Strauss and respected him highly as a composer and conductor, recalled that at this time Strauss was "enamoured" of the principal theme from *Guntram* and hummed it constantly. He wryly commented that ". . . unfortunately *Guntram* seems never to have been beloved by anyone other than its composer."

If this was a period of brilliant pianism in which the German-trained virtuosi held their own among all competitors, it was no less an era of the German virtuosi conductors. Besides Steinbach and Richard Strauss (at Bayreuth), there were Dr. Karl Muck (Berlin), Felix Mottl (Carlsruhe), Hans Richter (also at Bayreuth), Gustav Mahler (Vienna) and Artur Nikisch (Leipzig). Felix Weingartner was then at the beginning of his career. All of these conductors appeared at one time or another in Frankfurt and eventually Friedberg appeared as soloist with all of them.

Clara Schumann's last years were spent largely in a wheel chair, preferably in the garden when weather permitted. One of Friedberg's pupils (who studied with him at the end of the century) lived, as a child, in the house next door to Mme. Schumann and remembers her as a kind, good neighbor with a friendly smile and pleasant words for children. She recalls several of Brahms's visits, when the two great musicians sat on the open veranda, basking in the invigorating summer air and talking together. Since both were growing older and deaf they necessarily shouted to each other, their

30

interesting remarks overheard by the neighbors! Occasionally Brahms would go to the piano to play for Clara, at which moments the children pressed their ears close to the wall of her house to hear the music sounding through, sometimes faintly. "Perhaps *she* is playing now," they would whisper.

On May 20, 1896, Clara Schumann died, from the effects of a stroke suffered two months earlier. Buried in Bonn, it was there, at her funeral service, that Friedberg last saw Brahms, a somber, enigmatic, tragic figure. "Among the crowd of friends and fellow-musicians who followed the body of Clara Schumann to the cemetery," he recalled, "Brahms was at first conspicuously absent. Their friendship was already a legend. Brahms had been expected from Vienna, but the train was delayed and the services proceeded without him.

It was a beautiful day in May, warm, green and sunny and from a tree near the open grave a nightingale sang. Finally, Brahms arrived, his black hat pulled well down over his eyes, his face set, but without outward sign of emotion. Even when the earth revealed the coffin of Robert Schumann, and a great wave of emotion spread over the group, Brahms remained silent, immobile, outwardly unmoved. When mourners passed by, dropping earth into the grave, Brahms leaned forward, dropped three roses, then left hurriedly back to Vienna. "The hand of death was upon him at the time and he knew it," added Friedberg. "By April of the next year he, too, was gone." [7]

In this manner was the young musician parted from the two greatest musical influences of his life.

He was, however, not only to cherish the memories of Clara Schumann and Johannes Brahms, but he also pledged to hold aloft their idealism to the world.

Another interesting friend whose acquaintance Carl Friedberg made was Hugo Faisst, an amateur bass-baritone of professional caliber. Resident of Stuttgart, lawyer by profession, Faisst devoted his life and fortune to furthering

Hugo Wolf's career and sang his songs on every possible occasion. He even arranged at his own expense concerts at which other artists performed Wolf's songs. It was at Faisst's home in Stuttgart that Friedberg met Hugo Wolf.

There were then two societies dedicated to the propagation of Wolf's music—the Berlin and Vienna *Hugo Wolf Vereine*. Faisst founded, in 1898, the Stuttgart *Hugo Wolf Verein* at which Friedberg participated annually in concerts (several in the presence of the composer) until 1907. Besides Faisst, Friedberg appeared with Lula Mysz-Gmeiner, Karl Lang, Dr. Ludwig Wüllner and others in presenting all-Wolf programs.

Through Faisst's generosity Wolf moved into a large flat on the fourth floor of a house in Schwingasse, Vienna. Friedberg and Faisst often came to visit the composer and to go over his works with him. When together they gave the first performance of Wolf's songs to an invited audience in a recital hall in Vienna in 1900, or 1901, every famous singer immediately wished to engage Friedberg as an accompanying-artist. He subsequently accompanied Eugen Gura, Ernestine Schumann-Heink, Edith Walker, Elena Gerhardt and many others in *Lieder-Abende* (song recitals).

Having rounded out his academic studies and launched his career, especially as a teacher (an economic point he continually stressed to his students), Carl Friedberg now turned toward marriage. In 1901, at the age of 29, he married the youngest daughter of the British Consul-General at Frankfurt and to them were born four children—Curt, Hans, Stefan and Carola.

With his family responsibilities, (he still contributed to the support of his parents), the pianist, in addition to his teaching at the Frankfurt Conservatory, went every week to Mannheim, not far distant, where he taught from 1900-1904.

At the turn of the century musical concerts throughout Germany appeared to be increasing; the general public was taking an interest in concert-going which formerly was the pleasure of only a small group of music lovers. In Frankfurt alone, during the season 1900-1901, there were 36 grand symphonic concerts, 110 smaller orchestral concerts, 6 oratorio and 28 chambermusic concerts, without counting the opera and a great number of artists' and popular concerts.

Carl Friedberg was a part of this increased musical activity and the following several seasons were intensive ones for him, entailing much traveling. His annual tours of the German cities were climaxed by two Berlin recitals (March 2 and 11, 1904). Coldly received in the first, Friedberg was warmly acclaimed in the second when he followed d'Albert, Eduard Risler, Schnabel and Lhévinne, all of whom played recitals during the same week.

Among his orchestral (solo) engagements during this time may be noted his appearances at the *Allgemeiner Deutscher Music-Verein** which convened at Heidelberg in June, 1901 (Steinbach and Richard Strauss, conductors), where Friedberg was soloist in the Sgambati concerto. At the Frankfurt Museums Orchestra concerts he performed the César Franck *Symphonic Variations,* the Beethoven E flat and Mozart A Major concertos.

In May, 1902, Friedberg went with Hugo Heermann to Spain for a week of Beethoven's piano and violin sonatas, appearing in Madrid a few days before the wedding of King Alfonso XIII. Shortly after, he returned there with Johannes Hegar to perform the five Beethoven piano and cello sonatas. The two artists also presented the Beethoven works in Berlin, in 1904.

Friedberg's tours also took him to London where he gave a solo recital of works by Beethoven and Brahms in which he was warmly received for his interpretation. Back in Vienna, in two evenings of chamber music he performed with Professor de Conne the Beethoven "Kreutzer," Mozart G Major and Schumann D minor violin and piano sonatas.

* This society was founded around 1850 by Liszt in order to give contemporary composers performances of their works.

With Engelbert Roentgen he also played the five Beethoven cello sonatas.

Because of his growing reputation Friedberg was engaged as one of two soloists—Busoni was the other—for the Mannheim Festival of April 12-14, 1903, Felix Mottl, general music director, when the new festival hall was dedicated. This was Friedberg's first big festival appearance. Joachim was the featured violinist and the singers Johannes Messchaert, Berta Morena and Emilie Herzog were the vocal soloists. The first evening Friedberg performed the Brahms F minor Piano Quintet, with the Joachim Quartet. On the final evening he accompanied Jeannette Grumbacher-de Jong and Messchaert in a *Lieder* recital.

That same year (June 21-23) marked the celebration of the Twenty-Fifth Anniversary of the Hoch'sche Conservatorium. Distinguished delegates from the principal musical institutions of Germany and Switzerland, with Joachim at the head, assembled at Frankfurt. The career of one of the Frankfurt Conservatory's most notable exponents, Carl Friedberg, appeared almost to parallel the growth and development of this unique musical institution, for he had been closely associated with it for probably 18 of its 25 years: first, as a student, from approximately 1884-1892, and later as a teacher, from 1893-1904.

With the departure of James Kwast to Berlin in the fall of 1902, as teacher of the Advanced Class in Piano-playing at the Klindworth-Scharwenka Conservatory, Friedberg replaced his former teacher as pianist for the famous Frankfurter Trio, composed of Adolph Rebner, violinist, and Johannes Hegar, cellist—both of whom, like himself, were then members of the Frankfurt Conservatory faculty. In addition to a regular touring series of European concerts in the principal cities every year, the trio, throughout the winter season, presented Sunday afternoon concerts at the Conservatory every two weeks.

During the first season (1903-1904), in which Friedberg

was pianist, the trio performed works by Saint-Saëns, Mendelssohn, Brahms, Arensky, Dvorák, and introduced new trios by von Novak (an unknown), Wolf-Ferrari, as well as a *Sonata for Violin and Piano* by Volkmar Andreae, a Swiss composer-conductor.

In the fall of 1904 Friedberg was invited to head the Artists Class for Pianists at the Vienna Conservatory. At almost the same time, he was asked by Fritz Steinbach to fill a similar post at the Cologne Conservatory. Further, Steinbach offered a contract permitting him to choose his teaching hours. Since this contract gave more time for tours, he accepted Steinbach's offer.

His decision to leave Frankfurt was a matter of deep regret to both the music public and the critics. "One of the outstanding piano recitals of the season," wrote Hans Pfeilschmidt, "was by our excellent Carl Friedberg (he will, unfortunately, not be 'ours' much longer). His farewell program comprised works by Brahms, Bach and Waldemar Lütschg, all of which gave us much pleasure." [8]

In August, 1904, Friedberg moved to Cologne, ready to assume his new duties.

THE COLOGNE CONSERVATORY YEARS

(1904-1914)

Cologne, located on the left bank of the lower Rhine, originally an ancient Roman settlement founded in the Second Century B.C., was a much larger city than Frankfurt. At the time Carl Friedberg and his family came to live there, it was a thriving industrial city with a population of at least 500,000, noted for its exports of chocolate and the famous "eau de cologne." Its chief glories, then as now, are the imposing cathedral and the great, majestic river over which spans the reconstructed suspension bridges, connecting Cologne with Deutz.

Despite its religious heritage the "city of churches" also has its gay side, typified by the pre-Lenten Karneval, *Fastnacht,* when the whole city goes wild with joy; and by the unbridled wit of "Tünnes und Scheel," comic characters resembling somewhat "Mutt and Jeff." Although approximately eighty-five per cent of Cologne was destroyed in World War II, the city has been partially rebuilt and continues to foster the legendary Rhenish quality of its living: an appreciation for music, humor, friends, good food, and good wine.

In 1904 Cologne was half-circled by the Ring (boulevards), where were found some of the ancient fortifications, particularly several gates to the old free city: the Severintor, Hahnentor and the Eigelstein Tor.

On each side of the tree-lined boulevards were located the shops, offices and apartment houses of well-to-do people. South of the cathedral lies the narrow Hohestrasse, the main street of the city.

As in Frankfurt, the city's musical life centered around the opera, the symphony, the conservatory and its many choral groups. The opera was famous for its international repertory, while the historic Gürzenich symphony orchestra was devoted to standard symphonic literature.* Cologne alternated with Düsseldorf and Aachen in presenting the old Rheinische Music-Festival, the *Niederrheinisches Musikfest,* which always took place at Whitsuntide.

The Cologne Conservatory, founded in 1850, with Ferdinand Hiller as the first director, was originally known as the *Rheinische Musikschule.* Hiller was succeeded by Franz Wüllner in 1884 who, in turn, was followed by Fritz Steinbach, in 1902. At that time the conservatory ranked as one of the four leading music schools of Germany and, indeed, of the world, others being the Leipzig Conservatory, founded by Mendelssohn in 1843; the Berlin *Hochschule,* founded in 1869, of which Joachim was the first director; and the Frankfurt Hoch Conservatory, as we have noted, established in 1878.

The Cologne Conservatory * * was a large old-fashioned red sandstone building located at 7 Wolfsstrasse, a short, narrow street near the center of the city, with a recital hall similar in size and design to Carnegie Recital Hall in New York City. Carl Friedberg taught in a large studio on the top floor.

Now in his thirty-second year and renowned both as an

---

* The new opera house, located in another part of the city, is one of the most efficiently modern in Europe. The Gürzenich, only partially destroyed (in World War II) but now rebuilt, like the present city itself, is a curious hybrid of old and new architectural design.

** Reduced to a heap of rubble from the bombings of the city, the Conservatory (now known as the State Academy of Music) found other quarters in another part of the city.

artist and a teacher, Friedberg attracted to his Master Class pianists from all over Europe, England and America. At the time he joined the faculty the Conservatory consisted of 48 teachers and 549 students, 493 of whom were from Germany and 56 from foreign countries.

Prominent among the teachers were the pianists Isador Seiss (pupil of Clara Schumann's father) and Max van de Sandt (pupil of Liszt); the violinist, Bram Eldering (pupil of Joachim); and the cellist, Friedrich Grützmacher, Jr., who was later succeeded by Emanuel Feuermann.

Among the students in that year were the three Busch brothers, of whom Fritz and Adolf later had American careers, Elly Ney, Lonny Epstein, Willem van Hoogstraten, and Max Baldner, who later became the cellist of the Klingler Quartet.

At that time Friedberg used the Ibach piano exclusively. To encourage and stimulate young pianists to strive for higher artistic goals, he persuaded Rudolph Ibach, president of the Ibach firm, to offer annually a new concert grand to the outstanding piano student of the conservatory. Before a jury, hidden behind a screen so as not to be influenced by the personality of the players, the competing pianists performed with orchestra one of the lesser-known concertos which they had learned within a period of six weeks, without any help from their teachers. For the first award d'Albert's second *Concerto in E Major Op.* 12, was chosen as the competitive work. In succeeding years concertos by Emil Sauer and others were contest pieces.

Since he traveled extensively as performing pianist and returned to Frankfurt every two weeks to teach, Friedberg was unable to teach more than eight hours weekly at the Cologne Conservatory, as his contract stipulated. Steinbach, who was interested only in "results," gave him a free hand to arrange his days and hours of teaching as he wished.

Friedberg's fortnightly visits to Frankfurt thus enabled him to continue as pianist of the Frankfurter Trio. In addition he also performed with the Wendling Quartet (Stuttgart), the Bohemian Quartet (Leipzig), and the Gürzenich Quartet (Cologne).

His solo engagements that season included recitals at Heidelberg, Mannheim, Elberfeld, Berlin, Frankfurt, Düsseldorf, and other cities, where he was acclaimed for his "well-known pianistic bravura and rare interpretative ability." [1]

Steinbach, who had been a close friend of Brahms and was, therefore, an ardent "Brahmin," was not only the director of the Cologne Conservatory, but was also the conductor of the Gürzenich Concert Society Orchestra. For the tenth Gürzenich concert, in March 1905, Steinbach presented an all-Brahms program, conducting the chorus of the Society in "Nänie" (text by Schiller) and "Gesang der Parzen" (Goethe), followed by the D Major Symphony. "Then," wrote Paul Hiller, critic, "Carl Friedberg, who for about half a year has been active at the Cologne Conservatory, introduced himself with a masterful performance of the B flat Major piano concerto, for which one must welcome him joyfully as a new influential factor in the musical life of the Rhine." [2]

With the death of Isadore Seiss in September, 1905, his female students were placed with his former pupil, Elly Ney, while the male students were sent to Friedberg. By 1912 the latter's classes became so over-crowded—44 pupils a week—that Friedberg persuaded Steinbach to appoint as his assistant his young pupil, Lonny Epstein from Frankfurt.

Other members of Friedberg's Cologne Master Class who achieved prominence between 1904 and 1914 are Hans Bruch, nephew of the composer; Karin Elin Dayas, member of the faculty of the Cincinnati Conservatory of Music; Walter Golz, Professor of Music, Wilson College, Pennsylvania; Ernst Freudenthal and Erich Hammacher, both of whom became conductors; Ilse Fromm, talented composer-pianist, member of the faculty of the Hamburg Conservatory;

Erwin Schulhoff, gifted composer; Hans Haass; Franz Mittler, now living in New York City and member of the First Piano Quartet; Noel Straus, for many years a music critic on the staff of the New York *Times;* Paul Otto Möckel, later a teacher at the Zürich Conservatory, and Dr. Ernst Kunsemüller, Professor at the University of Kiel, who was killed in World War II.

The Bonn Chambermusic Festival, given in Beethoven Hall from May 21-25, 1906, with the Joachim Quartet as the participating ensemble, marked Friedberg's first of many appearances at this noted annual festival. With Joachim, he performed Beethoven's *Sonata Op.* 96 for violin and piano on the opening day and at the final concert "electrified the audience" with his performance of Schumann's *Symphonic Etudes.*

By 1906, German conductors were winning fame in America as well as in Europe and we note that Fritz Steinbach directed the last program of the New York Philharmonic season, while in the fall of the same year Dr. Karl Muck was appointed conductor of the Boston Symphony Orchestra.

That same season (1906-1907) marked the commencement of a new form of musical expression for Carl Friedberg —that of conducting.

Seeing that his own artist-students found it difficult to secure concert engagements from managers who, catering to public demand, booked "name artists" over "talented unknowns," Friedberg hit on something "spectacular" that would bring the young pianists to public attention and thus help remedy the situation.

With his students and several other young pianists he devised the plan of hiring noted ensembles such as the Winderstein Orchestra at Leipzig and the Berlin Symphony, for the purpose of presenting concerts in which the young talents would appear as soloists with their teacher as conductor.

At the first of these concerto concerts, given with the Winderstein Orchestra in Leipzig, December 18, 1906, Lonny Epstein performed three concertos: d'Albert's second in E Major, Mozart's C minor and Chopin's E minor.

The following evening, with the same orchestra, Elly Ney appeared under Friedberg's baton when she also presented three concertos: the Brahms B flat Major, Mozart C Major and Beethoven E flat Major.

Soon after, at Wiesbaden, in an all-Brahms concert at the Kurhaus, Elly Ney again performed the B flat concerto. "Her one-time teacher Carl Friedberg conducted it," wrote the critic Otto Dorn, "as well as the Haydn Variations and the E minor Symphony; he is not only a great educator and pianist, but also a safe and capable conductor." [3]

Having occupied an apartment on Vorgebirgstrasse for the first two years of his Cologne stay, it became necessary, as the family increased, for the artist to seek more spacious surroundings. The Friedbergs moved to a comfortable three-story white stone house in a residential suburb of the city, Lindenthal, which was to serve more or less as their permanent residence.

At the new house Friedberg chose a large room on the top floor for his studio, isolated from the rest of the household. Its floor was covered by a thick rug and the walls heavily insulated, so that he might practice any hour of the day or night. This need for privacy, quietude, and even solitude, in order that he might renew his inner resources so as to meet the rigorous schedule of concerts and teaching duties, was essential to the artist's well-being and happiness, and throughout his life remained an indispensable part of his daily living.

As early as 1907, critics began to compare Friedberg with d'Albert who for many years had been regarded as the top German pianist. In Krefeld, following the former's recital there on March 18, which apparently took place after one or more postponements, the critic of the local *Zeitung* wrote:

"Although we had heard Carl Friedberg in a concert of chambermusic with the Gürzenich Quartet his recent [solo] recital, in which he presented works of Beethoven, Schubert, Schumann and Chopin, made a deeper impression upon us. Friedberg would be much better known than he is now," the critic advised, "if he would not so often cancel his concerts." The discerning critic continued:

> One sees through his whole appearance that he is of a sensitive nature, an artist who greatly relies on moods. We may say of him that next to d'Albert, who has neglected his technic on account of his composing, no German pianist of the present day can bring such innerness of mind and soul or entice out of the keys so much poetry. One is held spellbound by his playing and completely forgets the instrument from which these beautiful sounds are brought. Whether he plays massive heavy chords, or weaves passages in tone that are like exquisite strings of pearls, or utters the most delicate sounds, this artist always makes everything he does exciting and deeply moving.[4]

In August of that year Friedberg enjoyed a happy holiday for three weeks as the guest of Mrs. Jay Gould at her magnificent summer home in Baden Baden—one of the few vacations he ever allowed himself. During this era Baden was one of the famous bath resorts, frequented by the most fashionable society and royalty. Among the internationally-famous guests who enjoyed Mrs. Gould's hospitality at the same time was Edward VII, King of England. Edward was a great lover of music, fond of devoting the social hour following dinner to hearing his favorite piano selections. During Friedberg's stay there he played almost daily for the King, offering in addition to classical "requests" his own inimitable improvisations. In private talks, the King prophetically remarked to the artist that unless his young nephew, William II, Emperor of Germany, were dissuaded from making undiplomatic speeches, the whole world would be thrown into turmoil. Edward also unsuccessfully attempted to persuade Friedberg to become head of the piano classes at the Royal College of Music in London, which he, as Prince of Wales, had founded in 1882. Thanking the King for his flattering offer the pianist replied that he was well satisfied with his present position at Cologne and that the damp London climate did not agree with his health.

Despite the pianist-teacher's busy career the Friedbergs were sociable and entertained frequently, especially following concerts. In addition to seeing much of their neighbors, the Steinbachs, and Grützmacher, the cellist who lived next door, such artists as d'Albert, Ysaye, Bronislaw Hubermann, Hugo Faisst, Hugo Becker, Walter Braunfels and many others made the Lindenthal house their headquarters while in Cologne. Other artists who called at the house when they came to the city for concert appearances were Busoni, Richard Strauss, Percy Grainger, Willy Hess, Karl Klingler, Hermann Abendroth, Franz von Vecsey, Arrigo Serato, Leonard von Zweygberg and Pablo Casals.

Following the pianist's concert with Ysaye at Cologne which took place on October 28, 1912, and which was heralded as one of the greatest artistic events in several years, the Friedbergs gave a dinner in honor of the noted violinist to which, among other guests, came Prince Carl von Hohenzollern and Princess Stephanie. After dinner the royal couple gave Friedberg an introduction to the Queen Mother of Belgium. Thereafter, on his several Belgian tours, Friedberg was to count among his audiences at Brussels members of the Belgian Royal Family.

Composers were also among the many visitors, often coming late at night to play their compositions and to hear Friedberg's opinion of their works, hopeful that he might include them in his recital programs. Among these may be

43

mentioned three composers, four of whose works Friedberg performed at Cologne with the Gürzenich Quartet: *Quintet in F Sharp Minor* by Ewald Straesser; *Trio in E Flat Major* by Volkmar Andreae; *Quintet in C Minor Op.* 64, and a *Piano Quartet in D Minor Op.* 113 by Max Reger.

Friedberg, who admired d'Albert above all pianists of his time, saw much of the noted composer-pianist when the latter's opera *Tragaldabas* was given its premiere at the Cologne opera house in November, 1908, with genuine success. d'Albert was a guest in Friedberg's house while the rehearsals were underway and the two musicians spent many hours talking together following late night rehearsals. Over a fine Havana cigar and coffee they discussed among other matters the progress of the rehearsals and the stage décor.

Because of his steadily growing interest in conducting and an increasing demand for recital appearances in various European countries, with more and more students clamoring for lessons, Friedberg gave up his role as pianist of the Frankfurter Trio with whom he had been associated from 1903-1908.

However, he continued to perform as assisting artist with many of the leading quartet ensembles, notably the Klingler Quartet at the (1909) Baden Baden Brahms Festival; the Rosé Quartet at the Munich Brahms Festival; the Rebner, Wendling, Heermann-Van Lier, and Bohemian quartets.

The 1909-1910 season was unusual in several respects. It marked the humorously-styled "Boston Invasion" of Cologne by a group of young American musicians who were touring the German conservatories with Wilhelm Heinrich of Boston. It was the season in which Friedberg made tours of both Italy and Belgium as soloist; and it was the year of the Chopin Centenary.

In 1910 Friedberg toured Italy as one of the soloists with the celebrated Cologne *Männerchor* (male chorus), conducted by J. Schwarz, appearing with them in Rome, Venice, Naples, Florence and Milan. The vocal soloist was

Plate 4
Carl Friedberg at the age of twenty

Plate 5

The Frankfurter Trio, 1902. Adolph Rebner, Carl Friedberg and Johannes Hegar

Mme. Hafgren Waag. Although Friedberg gave a piano group comprised of Chopin's "Ballade in F minor," Sgambati's "Nocturne No. 5," and two Liszt pieces ("Au bord d'une source" and the Paganini-Liszt "La Campanella") it was the Chopin piece and "Campanella" that won him the plaudits of the Rome audience. The following morning King Umberto and Queen Margarita summoned conductor and soloists to the palace where they were each awarded the highest Italian decoration.

On March 26, at Milan, where the tour ended, the choir and soloists visited the Home for Aged Musicians, established by Verdi in 1896, giving a brief concert for the many celebrated inmates; then proceeded to the grave of Verdi, where the choir sang a motet and placed a wreath of flowers on the great composer's grave, a tribute which greatly moved the Italian people.

Although Friedberg was first introduced to Brussels as the pianist of the Frankfurter Trio in 1907, he was not heard as solo-recitalist until the spring of 1910, when with a program comprised of works by Beethoven, Brahms, Chopin and Liszt (according to Felix Welcker) "he conquered the heart of the Brusslers by storm." [5] From this time on Friedberg was to hold the attention of the Belgian concert-going public which remained ever loyal and faithful to him.

For the hundredth anniversary of Chopin's birth, which was celebrated by many pianists who devoted entire programs to that composer's music, Friedberg, with Gerhard Tischer (editor of the *Rheinische Musikzeitung*), devised a program to interest the general public in the work of the Polish master which, as a part of the Chopin Festivals, they presented widely. The program was divided into two parts: Part I was a short address by Dr. Tischer on the subject of "Chopin: His Life and Work" after which, as Part II, Friedberg performed three groups of Chopin piano works arranged in the following order: 1. a) Ballade in G minor, b) Scherzo in B minor; 2. a) Etude in E Major *Op.* 10, b)

Valse in A minor, c) Etude in F Major *Op*. 25, d) Mazurka in B minor, e) Nocturne in F Sharp Major, f) Valse in A Flat Major; 3. a) Impromptu in F Sharp Major, b) Polonaise in A Flat Major. The B minor *Sonata* was a favorite of the pianist's and sometimes he substituted it for two of the groups.

Friedberg was now regarded as one of the top European teachers and wherever he appeared, in Germany, Switzerland, Belgium, Spain or England, he found young students waiting in his dressing-room, or at his hotel, eager for lessons. In some cities there were so many students seeking lessons that he often spent the remainder of the night teaching, getting to sleep for only an hour or two before taking the train to his next appearance. Indeed, it may be truly said of him that his love for teaching was so paramount that throughout his lifetime he placed the welfare of his pupils above his own health and career.

An essential part of Carl Friedberg's pedagogical personality was his sensitivity in recognizing specific talents of anyone who studied with him, and the ability to bring the material uniquely suited to each pupil's special gifts.

As an example of this ability may be mentioned the recitals of contemporary piano music given by Karin Elin Dayas. At Munich, Leipzig, Weimar and Cologne, Frl. Dayas performed works by Korngold, Reger, Weismann, Braunfels, Debussy, Ravel and Balakirew.

Encouraging some students to compose, Friedberg persuaded still others, in whom he discerned a conducting talent, to become conductors. At least two of his students occupied important symphonic posts: Dr. Ernst Kunsemüller, director of the Kiel Philharmonic; and Erich Hammacher, musical director at Trier.

Friedberg did not hesitate to add his artistic presence in concerts with his students if he thought a young pianist's career would be advanced. Nor did he fail to utilize any

46

and all opportunities for public performance to promote their musical interests.

Friedberg was still often away on concert tours, sometimes for weeks at a time. His students frequently found that he had traveled the entire night, in order to arrive in Cologne the next morning. From the station he came directly to the Conservatory. Taking only a slight pause for lunch, he taught straight through until evening.

Once when a pupil felt the symptoms of a cold and asked if he might postpone a scheduled orchestral rehearsal, Friedberg counselled him to attend the rehearsal, saying that later on the young pianist might have similar experiences but, nonetheless, must not cancel rehearsals or performances for such "inconsequential" excuses. "In that respect," he said, "we must discipline ourselves." However, in his concern, he sent the student home to rest in order that he might feel as well as possible for the rehearsal.

By 1910, Friedberg's concerts (inclusive of recitals, solos with orchestra, chamber music-player and conductor) had increased to sixty each season so that with his teaching at almost every stop (plus his Cologne teaching), he came into contact with an increasingly large number of would-be young artists and teachers. His influence, therefore, spread over the entire continent. He not only heard and criticized the younger artists' playing but also talked with them about the problems of their careers, discussing with them the artistic climate of the locality in which they worked and how it might be improved. One familiar complaint was the same wherever he went: the "new crop" of young pianists could not secure artistic employment from the managers because the latter were interested only in pushing "name artists" for whom they could command large fees. Realizing the seriousness of the problem, Friedberg wrote, in what is believed to be his first preserved writing, a letter addressed to his own concert manager.

47

"The artist who, for the first time, desires to appear before an audience entrusts you completely with his artistic business affairs; in fact he *must* do so. You are then the agent between the artist and the public and therefore it is to you that I make the following proposal:

"In order to avoid unnecessary wastes of both time and money on the part of concert managers, young artists, and conductors, I suggest that there be arranged every year in the more important towns and cities musical events which may be termed 'Try-out Concerts.' You, together with a jury appointed by you as unbiased as possible, select from a group of young artists those who have an indisputable claim to recognition not only for their talent and proficiency, but also for the impression they are able to make on their audiences. To these 'Try-out Concerts' should be invited the public, critics, and, most important of all, conductors and the Board of Directors of the larger concert societies. Conductors will especially appreciate this manner of getting acquainted with young talents, encountering them for the first time directly in front of an audience. Thus private auditions of the artists with the conductors, so unsatisfactory and so time-consuming for both, are eliminated.

"To cover the expenses of these 'Try-out Concerts' you should be able to obtain an annual contribution from all of the artists whom you represent and are likely to represent in the future. I am sure that you will not meet with any refusal. Eventually, a contract with an artist might be made dependent on the condition of his making a contribution toward these expenses. Anyway it would be worth-while to find out by an inquiry of leading personalities the general reaction to this proposal. Independent of financial considerations the selection among the younger generation would be made faster than hitherto and prove undoubtedly more

48

reliable and suitable to the needs and wishes of the conductors throughout the country." [6]

Whether the Wolff management gave this reasonable letter any consideration is not known; but the letter itself is a concrete example of Friedberg's unselfish attitude toward his younger colleagues and certainly the plan he proposed must be regarded as a forerunner of present day contests.

By 1913, Friedberg's reputation had so greatly increased that Gerhard Tischer said of him: "Were I asked whom I consider the greatest living pianist since d'Albert has left off playing in public, I would answer without hesitation: Carl Friedberg, and I would justify this opinion with the incomparable charm of his touch and with the universality of his playing, the style of which does justice to the greatness of Bach and Beethoven as well as to the most intimate art of Chopin, or the tingling virtuosity of Liszt.

"Friedberg's playing makes one forget the purely mechanical part,—he easily overcomes all technical difficulties—and so is able to carry his public into higher spiritual spheres. Poetry is the essence of his art.

"Those who know this artist know how vivid are his interests, how his intelligence takes part in all questions of cultural work and how the largeness of his mind prevents his one-sidedness. He has an outstanding knowledge of musical literature, thanks to a phenomenal memory and whenever anything new appears he takes up his position toward it. This is what makes him such a wonderful model for his pupils; he shows them that a real artist must necessarily be a well-educated individuality. He can at any minute give them explanations and examples not only from the literature of the piano, but also from orchestral and dramatic pieces, from songs and chambermusic. Here we meet the same universality which is the chief characteristic of Friedberg's artistic greatness." [7]

Not yet forty the pianist was a unique combination of the serious artist-teacher and devotee of good living. Now, with an almost ascetic, refined yet kindly countenance, his hair beginning to recede from his broad, dome-like forehead, he presented the picture of the man of culture *per se*. He was, in addition, a marvelous raconteur of both imaginative and humorous stories, an authority on the finest foods and wines.

Besides Richard Strauss, whose opera *Der Rosenkavalier* received its premiere that season, Max Reger and Hans Pfitzner were the three most talked of composers in Germany in 1911. All three men were friends of Friedberg and he, unlike many pianists who confined themselves to the standard repertory of piano works, had frequently performed new works by all of them. He had also invited Pfitzner to write a piano concerto for him, but circumstances occurring in the next several years were to prevent the completion of this work until 1922.

Notwithstanding the fact that critics and the general public alike often rejected new works, Friedberg was determined to include the compositions of contemporary composers in his programs whether these works were liked or not; for he was convinced that there could be no continuous musical progress from one generation to another without the living composer's having his opportunity to be heard.

Among highlights of his concert activities between 1910 and 1914, during which Friedberg's appearances increased to more than eighty engagements in both 1913 and 1914, must be mentioned several Berlin recitals. In January, 1911, at Beethoven Hall, for the first time, he won praise from all critics. In February, 1912, Friedberg, Artur Schnabel and Mark Hambourg gave Berlin recitals during the same week.

During his increased visits to Berlin Friedberg met among others Ossip Gabrilowitsch and his wife, Clara Clemens, Mark Twain's daughter; the Viennese composer Arnold Schönberg whose music was beginning to create a stir in Berlin; and Fritz Kreisler who, after fifteen years of concert-giving, had become the most celebrated violinist in Berlin. Here he also met Godowsky, Ernest Hutcheson, Josef

Lhévinne. Later, in America, he was to become well acquainted with all these artists.

In 1912, the Friedbergs made a trip to Leipzig by automobile with the Steinbachs to celebrate with a "surprise party," the sixtieth birthday of the painter and sculptor, Max Klinger, who had created the Beethoven monument in that city. Among others present were the poet, Morgenstern, and Eulenberg, musical publisher in Leipzig.

In the summer of 1913, Friedberg was booked for another tour of Belgium and, for the first time Holland, where he played several recitals and made orchestral (solo) appearances in Brussels, Ghent, Amsterdam, Rotterdam and other cities. At The Hague, where he gave two recitals (following his recovery from the indisposition for which Myra Hess substituted for him,) *De Telegraaf* commented: "The eminent artist, a thinker, a dreamer, and a truly poetic interpreter at the piano, offered us unforgettable experiences and awakened each time stormy enthusiasm." [8] So great was his reception by Dutch audiences that he returned to Holland during the following January, where he played fourteen concerts in fourteen days. He was especially in demand for his interpretations of Beethoven's *Sonata Op.* 109, Chopin's B minor *Sonata,* and Schumann's *Kreisleriana* and *Toccata.*

Everywhere Friedberg was spontaneously acclaimed. At Frankfurt and Karlsruhe, Franz Zweich said ". . . we count Friedberg among the first representatives of his instrument"; at Leipzig his Beethoven recital was "exalted and unforgettable"; at Munich, Dresden, Heidelberg, Vienna, Prague, Stuttgart, the reports were the same.[9] On April 7, 1914, the artist had the honor of appearing at a Soirée as recitalist before the Crown Prince and Crown Princess. At Bonn, during the last big Beethoven Festival before World War I, the hall was so overcrowded during his recital that several hundred people were seated on the stage.

Friedberg's solo appearances with orchestra were so numerous that we can only suggest their geographical scope and indicate which concertos conductors sought most to have him perform. From the time of his debut with Gustav Mahler and the Vienna Philharmonic in 1892, up to 1914, a period of twenty-two years, Friedberg had performed with virtually every orchestra of note in Europe. Among the most important were appearances with the Berlin Philharmonic and the Leipzig Gewandhaus, (both under the direction of Nikisch); the Dresden Court Orchestra (Richard Strauss); the Gürzenich Orchestra, Cologne (Steinbach); the Strasbourg Orchestra (Pfitzner); the Vienna Konzertverein (Ferdinand Löwe); the Städtiche Kurverwaltung, Wiesbaden (Carl Schuricht); the Hamburg Orchestra (Klemperer); the Queen's Hall Orchestra, London (Sir Henry Wood); the Colonne, Lamoureux, and Chevillard orchestras, Paris; the Concerts Ysaye, Brussels; the Concertgebouw, Amsterdam (Mengelberg); and the Madrid Philharmonic. Following his orchestral appearance at Madrid, in 1913, Friedberg received the highest honor ever conferred upon an artist there, when he was created a "Knight of Isabella Catolica."

In Germany, Austria, Italy, Spain, Belgium, Holland and Switzerland Friedberg was most in demand for the Brahms, Beethoven, Schumann, Mozart, Tschaikovsky and Liszt concertos; also the César Franck *Symphonic Variations.*

With the Colonne, Lamoureaux and Chevillard orchestras in Paris, the Concerts Ysaye in Brussels, and the Queen's Hall orchestra in London, he was in demand for performances of contemporary works such as the Debussy *Fantasy in G Major,* Rachmaninoff *Concerto in F Sharp Minor,* Strauss *Burleske* and the Busoni Piano Concerto *Op.* 39.

Of the pianist's (1913) Leipzig performance of the Brahms B flat *Concerto* the local *Tageblatt* stated: "The performance of the Brahms work released a veritable storm of enthusiasm which rose to a frenzy of excitement. And no wonder, since two of the most prominent German artists contributed to the effect of the whole: Artur Nikisch and Carl Friedberg, the former as Brahms' conductor, the latter

52

as Brahms' pianist, and one whose equal would be hard to find." [10]

While Friedberg first became known as a conductor with his series of piano concerto concerts in which he presented his pupils and other young artists as soloists, his activities as a conductor were not limited to this function. Besides conducting the Leipzig, Cologne and Berlin orchestras, he also conducted the Concerts Ysaye in Brussels during the 1912-1913 spring season when Ysaye was absent in America.

At Frankfurt, on April 7, 1913, in the large hall of the Saalbau, Friedberg substituted for Carl Schuricht when he conducted the Ruehl Choral Society in a performance of Mozart's *Dominum* and Brahms' *German Requiem*.

Friedberg also had aspirations to conduct opera, though opportunities in this field were rare; for all the opera-houses maintained a staff of conductors, any one of whom was ready to step in at the moment there was need for replacement. Nevertheless, he conducted at least one performance of *Walküre* at St. Gallen, Switzerland, and read through the score of Debussy's *Pelléas et Mélisande* with the composer in the expectation of conducting that work in Germany. He also gave at Cologne the first performance there of Hugo Wolf's *Der Feuerreiter,* to a text by Edward Mörike, the German poet, Ballad for Chorus and Orchestra.

In the wake of his many diversified European triumphs, it was announced that the artist would make his first American tour in the fall of 1914.

53

IV

THE WORLD WAR I YEARS AND AFTERMATH

(1914-1922)

For the season 1914-1915 Carl Friedberg was scheduled for concert tours in both Russia and the United States, the American tour to be undertaken under the management of his sister, Annie Friedberg who, since 1912, had become active in the music managerial field in New York City.

When the pianist left Germany during the first week in July 1914, there was no indication of unrest, or of the impending conflict. He fulfilled concert dates in Paris and in other French cities and made a tour of the Netherlands. On the evening of July 29, he gave a recital at Scheveningen (Holland), when he first learned of the strained state of diplomatic relations among the European countries. Upon inquiring whether it was safe to return to Paris, Friedberg was assured by the German attaché that affairs appeared to be proceeding normally and that there was no immediate prospect of war. However, on returning to the French capital, the situation had deteriorated so rapidly that he found banks and stores closed, trains off schedule, and the streets filled with excited people.

Acting on impulse, he took an automobile for the seaport town, Dieppe, where in a drenching rain he spent the night on the quay, without umbrella, galoshes, or a change of clothes. In his haste to get to a neutral country and so proceed to America for his scheduled tour, he was forced to abandon all his belongings in Paris. At Dieppe, crowds trying to get to England were so great that three shiploads crossed the channel that night. By the ruse of giving Switzerland instead of Germany as his birthplace, Friedberg persuaded the French officers to allow him to board the last ship leaving the port.

In London, affairs did not proceed smoothly. Friedberg was recognized as the famed German pianist and taken into custody as a prisoner of war, on parole. He was not permitted to go more than five miles in any direction from the little house in Sydenham, outside London, where he was staying, yet within that area he had almost unlimited freedom. Here his English friends, Donald Tovey, Percy Grainger, Sir Edward Elgar and others visited him.

Restricted for eight weeks, Friedberg upon application to the British Home Secretary by a friend, a Member of Parliament, was released under a special permit that enabled him to proceed to New York.

Traveling via the White Star Liner "Celtic" which left Liverpool on September 30, the pianist was the only German passenger aboard. The ship docked in New York City on October 8. Soon after his arrival he was tendered a reception at the Hotel Astor by the German Press Club, where he was presented to the large assemblage by his sister-manager, Annie.

For his Carnegie Hall debut, on November 2, he offered a program which consisted of the "G minor Organ Prelude and Fugue" (Bach-Liszt), *Sonata in E Major Op.* 109 (Beethoven), *Etudes Symphoniques* (Schumann), three Brahms pieces; "Ballade in G minor." *Op.* 118, "Intermezzo in E Flat Major" *Op.* 117, "Rhapsody in E Flat Major" *Op.* 119, and a final Chopin group: "Ballade in G minor," "Waltz in C sharp minor," "Etude" (from *Op.* 10, *No.* 4) and "Polonaise in F sharp minor."

Friedberg won the acclaim of both audience and press with H. E. Krehbiel of the *Tribune,* one of the most noted critics of his day, commenting that the pianist "gave a pure and high pleasure by his playing. He reads his music aright, and he knows how to make his vehicle eloquent. He does not outrage it in an effort to astound, nor degrade it through a desire to make it contribute to mere 'lascivious pleasings.' Euphony, clarity of utterance, varied gradation of dynamics marked the mechanical part of his playing of everything . . . and he had a deep feeling for the emotional conceits as well as their aesthetic beauty." [1]

Solo recitals followed in Boston, Chicago, Cincinnati and smaller mid-western cities where Friedberg was enthusiastically received. His orchestral (solo) appearances that season included performances with the Cincinnati Symphony, Ernst Kunwald,* conductor, with which orchestra he performed the Brahms second concerto; the St. Louis Symphony (Max Zach), with which he gave "a monumental performance" of the Schumann concerto; and the New York Philharmonic (Josef Stransky) with which he repeated the Schumann concerto, performing this work, according to the New York *Post,* ". . . not only correctly and beautifully, but entertainingly, thus coming up to all of Hans von Bülow's standards for pianists." [2]

Among other artists who appeared with the New York Philharmonic that season were the singers: Lucrezia Bori, Alma Gluck, Julia Culp, and Pasquale Amato; the violinists: Fritz Kreisler, Efrem Zimbalist, Arrigo Serato, and Jacques Thibaud; the pianists: Ferruccio Busoni, and Ossip Gabrilowitsch.

The January 2, 1915 issue of *Musical America* brought forth an article written by Harriette Brower, in the form of an interview, which gives considerable insight into the

* Formerly conductor of the Berlin Philharmonic.

artistic personality of Friedberg and his attitude toward music and teaching.

CARL FRIEDBERG

"After listening to Carl Friedberg, both in recital and with orchestra, it was a pleasure to have the opportunity for a talk with him in the seclusion of the home; to find him the simple, unaffected gentleman, with frank, winning manner, quite willing to talk of his methods of teaching and of study.

" 'I might say at the outset,' began the pianist, 'that I believe the *legato* touch is of the utmost importance in piano playing; it is the *sine qua non* of beautiful tone. I am aware that some modern players do not agree with this: they think everything should be played with the arm. Even Busoni, whom I admire exceedingly and consider one of the very greatest artists, says in his edition of Bach's *Well-Tempered Clavichord* that there is no *legato* possible on the piano. I must differ from those who hold to this idea, for I emphatically believe and can prove there is a *legato* on the piano. It is the foundation of beautiful tone.

EXPRESSIVE TONE

" 'The tone an artist draws from his instrument should be round, full and expressive, capable of being shaded and varied, just as is the *bel canto* of the singer. We should learn to sing with our fingers. I knew the famous singer and teacher Stockhausen and played much for him. From this artist I learned a great deal, which helped me to acquire a singing, expressive tone on the piano.

" 'I endeavor to give my piano tone the quality of the singing voice. For this reason I have made myself familiar with a large number of operas of every school. When quite a young lad I learned *Tristan und Isolde* by heart, and I still know it, and many other opera scores.

" 'I have been largely my own teacher, though in the beginning I had most excellent instruction [from James Kwast and Clara Schumann]. I also received suggestions from Anton Rubinstein. When I played for him as a youth, he expressed himself as especially pleased with my singing tone and my manner of using the pedals. I deeply appreciated his words of commendation.

" 'Together with much concert work, I have done a great deal of teaching. For the last ten years I have been located in Cologne, at the Conservatory, where I had charge of the artist class. It takes the form of a *Meister Schule,* along the same lines as the one in Vienna over which Godowsky used to preside.

" 'In my teaching I begin with finger training, for I am not one who believes in neglecting this side of piano technic. If you will come over to the piano I will show you just what I mean.' The artist seated himself at the keyboard, illustrating as he talked.

HAND POSITION

" 'I first require a correct position. In this I follow the advice of Rubinstein, who counseled the student to sit on a chair which would be the right height to keep the level of the arm and wrist, not allowing the elbow to hang below the keyboard. The knees are to be close together; the heels planted on the floor, with the soles of the feet resting on the pedals, but not depressing them. The arms fall easily at the side, as Mme. Schumann taught, but not pressed against it. Now the hand is placed on five consecutive keys. I will now hold my hand in this position, and depress one key with the middle finger. As you see, the condition of the arm is quite loose and relaxed. You can move my arm back and forth, or in any direction you choose, but it will be impossible for you to dislodge my finger from the key, for it remains there with full relaxed arm weight.

" 'I now begin to make various movements to render the fingers flexible and independent. When they are somewhat under control I begin to train the thumb under the hand, ready for scale playing. The thumb moves under the hand as soon as it has left its key and is held under the hand until its turn comes to play. I am a great believer in thorough scale practice in all forms.

" 'In regard to equalizing the fingers, some players struggle to make all fingers equally strong; yet with all their effort the fourth finger can never be made as vigorous as the thumb. And why should all the fingers be equal— one just the same as the others? It is not necessary. Just those slight inequalities of touch give variety and expressiveness to the playing. There are times when it is better to use weaker fingers than strong ones.

" 'For all this technical drill I use hundreds of exercises of my own, which have never been printed. I do not adhere strictly to one set of these, but invent new ones constantly, perhaps changing them every week. If fingers are weak and bending, they must be made strong by special pressing and gymnastic exercises.

LEGATO TOUCH

" 'The student concentrates his efforts on *legato* touch and on beautiful and expressive tone quality. If I have a melody to play I can do it, as many modern artists do, with a movement of hand and arm for each note—that is to say, detaching one note from another. With proper pedaling, such a manner of playing can be made to sound very well.' Here Mr. Friedberg illustrated his point. 'Now I will play the same passage with pure *legato* touch and you will hear the difference. I prefer the pure *legato* to the detached way of playing. When a melody lies in more extended position, the hand can reach for the notes with steadiness and control. We might liken this tense reaching out from one note to another to a suspension bridge, swung between two supports—the fingers.

" 'I believe in making everything musical, in always making the tone beautiful, even in technical exercises and scales,' continued the pianist. 'The piano is more than a thing of metal and wood; it can speak, and the true artist will draw from it wonderful tones. It should be part of his constant study to create beautiful tone. I believe a single tone can be made expressive. I can prove this to you.' Here Mr. Friedberg played single tones here and there on the keyboard. Each of these was played with arm weight. The pressure was slightly relaxed after the key had sounded, not enough to remove the finger, but just sufficient to make the tone expressive and in that way achieve a variety in quality and color. The tone *sang*.

" 'It is a most interesting study, this effort to discover new and beautiful effects of tone and variety of production. So much can be done with *staccati*, too. There are so many kinds: the hand *staccato*, the finger *staccato*, the drawing off, elastic touch. *Staccato* can sometimes be executed with a single finger, for an entire passage, as this for example.' Here the pianist dashed into a passage in eighth notes, from a Chopin mazurka [probably *Op. 7, No. 4*], using only the second finger and keeping the rest of the hand closed. He then repeated the selection with normal fingering and *legato* touch; the contrast was very marked.

"If a student comes to you, I asked, who plays tolerably well, though not trained along these technical lines, do you require him, first of all, to go through this technical drill?

" 'I do not require it. I explain my ideas to him, illustrate them and show him the advantage of such training. He is at once anxious to study in this way; I have never found one who did not wish to do so.' " [3]

Friedberg's second New York recital took place in January, 1915, at Aeolian Hall. The program comprised the *Thirty-two Variations in C minor* and "Les Adieux" *Sonata* (Beethoven); *Scenes from Childhood* (Schumann); and groups of pieces by Brahms and Chopin.

A. Walter Kramer wrote that ". . . the large audience, which included many distinguished artists, was loath to leave and after calling the pianist out a dozen times induced him to add Schubert's D Major Rondo." [4]

Maintaining his attitude of neutrality, for the pianist was opposed to war on any grounds, he appeared in February with Lucy Marsh, soprano, and Loyal Phillips Shawe, baritone, in a concert at Providence, the proceeds of which were given to the Rhode Island Belgian-Relief Fund. He also performed in similarly arranged concerts with Anna Case, soprano, and Arrigo Serato, violinist.

In March he appeared in a New York concert given under the auspices of Count von Bernstorff and Dr. Constantin Dumba, ambassadors respectively of Germany and Austria, for the benefit of the German and Austro-Hungarian reservists.

For the February meeting of "The Bohemians," at Lüchow's, a famous German restuarant, Friedberg gave, with Edouard Dethier, violinist, the first local performance of Dohnányi's *Sonata in C sharp minor Op.* 21. The pianist also played a solo contemporary group which included two short works of his own: "Gavotte al 'Antico" and "Petite Etude."

Summing up the successes of his first American season, *Musical America* stated that the pianist's "triumphs during his first concert tour indicate that he has established himself firmly as a factor in the musical life of America." [5]

Owing to the chaotic conditions abroad Friedberg who, in 1914, was divorced from his wife, made arrangements to spend the summer in America and to devote some of his time to teaching. His international fame as a teacher had preceded him here and when it was announced that he would teach during the summer of 1915, he received many applications from young pianists in various parts of the United States.

The pianist's second American tour was varied by his appearances as assisting-artist with the Kneisel Quartet in Boston, New York, Chicago and other cities, performing the Richard Strauss *Quartet for Piano and Strings,* and joining with Willem Willeke, cellist of the quartet, to play the little-known Chopin cello and piano *Sonata Op. 65.*

His solo recital tour, beginning in Indianapolis and continuing to Buffalo, Chicago, Galesburg, Illinois, took him as far west as Lincoln, Nebraska and Appleton, Wisconsin; south to Washington, D. C., Knoxville, Tennessee and Macon, Georgia.

During that season Friedberg gave only one New York recital, an all-Beethoven program comprising two sonatas: *Op.* 90; *Op.* 27 *No.* 2; four "Bagatelles" and the "Rondo in G Major," *Op.* 129. Critics in general agreed that never before had they heard Beethoven's piano works ". . . more illuminatingly, more eloquently, more movingly interpreted." The *Sun* remarked that ". . . where it took 350 people to give a recent Beethoven Festival uptown, Carl Friedberg in Aeolian Hall yesterday afternoon showed what one man could do with an all-Beethoven programme, and did it uncommonly well." [6]

In addition to giving his services for various war relief agencies, on numerous occasions the noted German pianist gave of his great art to aid struggling political causes and to support American charities. Typical of his artistic generosity may be cited his appearances at the home of Mrs. Samuel Untermeyer, at Graystone on the Hudson, with Metropolitan Opera singers Herman Weil and Caroline Ortman for the benefit of the American Suffrage Party; and at Paterson, New Jersey, where he performed with Alice Nielson, soprano, and Wassily Besekirsky, Russian violinist, in a concert to aid local hospitals.

The artist's success during his first two seasons had been so remarkable that it had recalled to one critic the triumphant tour of Anton Rubinstein, many years before. "Probably no pianist in the last decade has been more favorably received than has Carl Friedberg," wrote *Musical Courier.*[7]

The pianist had originally intended to remain in America only temporarily, but with the spread of the conflict to other countries, it became impossible for him to return to Europe.

This fact realized, Frank Damrosch, Founder and Director of the New York Institute of Musical Art, engaged Friedberg as teacher of the Advanced Students of Piano, beginning with the fall session, September, 1916. In that same year the artist married his second wife, Gerda von Wätjen.

The Friedbergs spent the following two summers in Seal Harbor, Maine, where they formed part of a distinguished group of musical artists, which included Fritz and Harriet Kreisler, Harold Bauer, Josef Hofmann, Frank and Walter Damrosch, Olga Samaroff, Leopold Stokowski, Ossip Gabrilowitsch and his wife Clara Clemens, Karl Muck, Carlos Salzedo, Ernest Schelling and Franz Kneisel.

Under war-time conditions, with many of these artists unable to return to their homelands, there developed an intimate friendship, or camaraderie, which could not have otherwise existed; for all were united in mutual concern over the fate of Europe.

The invigorating air of the Maine sea-coast town together with its lakes, deep forests and dark paths through which the artists strolled, proved to be an ideal spot for practicing and teaching, and from every open window could be heard the sound of piano, violin, or other stringed instrument. The little steamer from Ellsworth brought one piano after another from Boston or New York.

In this atmosphere there was no rush or hurry of any kind; nobody had a care in the world. Following the day's activities one met one's friends at Jordan Pond for tea or dinner. In the evening there were informal meetings at the homes of the various artists where each played for the others, talked of music, compared tempi. Friedberg always remembered one evening in the home of Gabrilowitsch when during a long, terrifying thunderstorm, the house lit only by candles, because power lines were down, Gabrilowitsch played Beethoven sonatas all through the night to calm his frightened friends.

At Kreisler's request that Friedberg arrange transcriptions of short piano works to add to the violin's meager concert repertory, he transcribed seven short pieces for violin and piano from composers of the Seventeenth and Eighteenth centuries. These were "Andante Cantabile" and "Pan and Syrinx" by Michel de Monteclair; "Old French Gavotte" (Author Unknown); "Adagio in E Flat Major" by Mozart; "Rondo in D Major" by Schubert; "Menuet" by Haydn and "Slavonic Lament" by E. Schuett. Kreisler added bowing marks and violin fingerings to these pieces, which were then published by Carl Fischer. During this same summer the two artists "tried out" the new pieces in a benefit concert given in a small church at Seal Harbor, Maine.

Although members of the artists' colony were engaged in serious work they sometimes relaxed in lighter moods, which gained the male pianist members the epithet, "The Convict Group," bestowed on them by an irreverent visitor.

The story, according to the Chicago *Musical Leader*, had its beginning when Gabrilowitsch suddenly decided to shave his head. The moment he appeared in public ". . . with a pate like an incandescent globe," Stokowski, to the delight of his friends and the grief of his wife, also "sacrificed his hair on the altar of comfort." Then Harold Bauer exchanged his bushy mane for "a crop of closely cropped pin-feathers."

On a week-end outing aboard a private yacht, the above-mentioned artists were celebrating their newly-discovered scalps when Carl Friedberg walked into their midst, his hair flowing in the breeze. Acting on concerted inspiration the three shorn ones pounced upon the newcomer and prepared to remove his hair by force, but Friedberg was equal to the occasion. He produced a contract which stated that he was booked to play during the summer, and his plea that "Hair is an absolute essential to artistic success," was sufficiently convincing to stay the hands of the would-be barbers.

At this moment Josef Hofmann appeared with his customary business-like trim. The hairless trio immediately brandished their shears but his eloquent pleas of delicate health, the responsibilities of fatherhood, and the explanation that the artistic printed matter bearing his normal likeness would have to be revised if his appearance were altered, saved his hair. Fritz Kreisler was the next "victim" but with tears in his eyes and with mock trembling hands he pointed to his recently healed war wounds and a surge of sympathy was awakened within the hearts of his would-be "assailants." Prolonged applause from the assembled guests greeted the three artists who, in this manner, were able to preserve their natural adornments.[8]

The season of 1916-1917 was unusual in several respects in that it brought Friedberg and Kreisler together in joint recitals; it was the season of the pianist's first appearance with the Boston Symphony Orchestra; it was the beginning of his long teaching affiliation at New York's famed Institute of Musical Art; and finally, with the coming of spring, it marked the entry of the United States into the world conflict on the side of the Allies. This latter turn of events was temporarily to stifle art in both America and Europe, bringing to an abrupt halt the progress of Friedberg's career and that of other artists of alien nationality.

The two great international artists, Kreisler and Friedberg, first appeared together in October, at Paterson, New Jersey, where they were enthusiastically received for their performances of Beethoven's "Kreutzer" *Sonata* and the newly-arranged pieces for violin and piano by Friedberg.

Besides these works Friedberg played a group of short pieces by Brahms, Schubert, Schumann and Chopin, while Kreisler was heard in the Conus concerto and a group of his own familiar arrangements, the accompaniments played by Carl Lamson. As an encore Friedberg played the familiar F minor "Moment Musicale" by Schubert. As soon as he had finished, Kreisler appeared on stage and played the same piece in his own arrangement for violin and piano, much to the delight of the audience.

When the two artists performed in Boston, "Symphony Hall was packed to the doors," wrote the *Traveler*. The program featured the César Franck *Sonata for Piano and Violin* and the Friedberg violin and piano arrangements which they ". . . performed superbly and for which they were tumultuously acclaimed." [9]

In December, in a sold-out concert at Carnegie Hall, New York, the two artists repeated the same program with the exception of the sonata, performing instead of the Franck, the Brahms G Major Sonata.

Max Smith wrote that Kreisler knew full well when he generously invited Friedberg to share honors with him in the Brahms Sonata and in the pianist's transcriptions of classic pieces that he was dealing with a true, sincere and exceedingly accomplished artist. "To hear Brahms's beautiful sonata as played by those two distinguished men was a delight from first to last," wrote Smith. "The modest little man at the piano who subsequently, in the music he had adapted so effectively, shrunk from acknowledging the applause with his partner, by no means filled a subordinate role in the inspiring results achieved. Indeed, there were some persons in the auditorium who, though fully alive to the eloquence of Kreisler's cantilena in the flowing melody wherein Brahms has incorporated his 'Regenlied,' felt that Friedberg showed more profound and intense sympathy with the spirit of the composer than his collaborator. His performance of the piano part, so exquisitely elaborated in nuance, so incisively expressive in every phrase, was nothing short of masterly." [10]

By popular demand the two artists were heard again three weeks later in Carnegie Hall, where they featured the Franck *Sonata*. It is to be regretted that circumstances beyond the control of the two great musicians prevented their further joint concerts—a collaboration which had brought joy not only to themselves, but also to a large and enthusiastic public.

During the same month Friedberg was invited to arrange an all-Brahms program for the first concert of the season in the series given by the Society of the Friends of Music. Together with Artur Bodanzky, musical director of the Friends (who was also the leading conductor of the German repertory at the Metropolitan Opera) he rehearsed the quartet of singers who performed six unfamiliar quartets and the *Zigeunerlieder*. The singers were Elsa Alves, Gerda von Wätjen Friedberg, Paul Draper and Rheinhold von Warlich. Friedberg not only accompanied the singers in the concert but also gave a solo Brahms group.

That season the pianist was most in demand for his playing of the Schumann concerto, which work he performed with the New York Symphony Society (Walter Damrosch), the Cincinnati Symphony (Kunwald), and the Boston Symphony (Muck), playing this work not only in Boston but also on tour with the orchestra in Baltimore, Washington, D. C., and other Southern cities. Muck also engaged the pianist for a second appearance in Boston later during the same season, at which time Friedberg gave his incomparable reading of the Brahms B Flat Major Concerto. Olin Downes wrote that ". . . not in seventeen years at these [Boston] concerts has this concerto been so superbly presented." [11] In the same concert Ernest Bloch, who had recently arrived in America, conducted his "Three Jewish Poems."

With the United States' aid to the Allied Cause in sending large shipments of clothing, iron, steel, and especially coal to the invaded countries, Americans themselves began to feel the pinch of privation. The sight of audiences sitting in unheated concert halls in their coats and wrapped in blankets became a familiar one, while pianists and other instrumentalists resorted to hot water bottles and heating pads, in order to keep fingers warm until they actually appeared on stage.

It was under such uncomfortable circumstances that Carl Friedberg played his last New York recital for several years in January 1917, at Aeolian Hall, where he was heard in a program of works by Schumann and Chopin.

That season he made both a Mid-Western and Southern tour which took him to Toledo (where he was always greatly beloved as an artist and man), St. Louis, and other cities, and as far south as Louisville, Kentucky, where he gave a joint recital with his wife.

Meanwhile, the war hysteria that had gripped America gradually worsened despite strong protests from artists, musicians, and a few sane laymen, with the result that anti-German sentiment became so strong the Metropolitan Opera was forced to cancel production of German opera. Beethoven, Brahms, Schumann and other German composers were denied their rightful places on symphonic and recital programs.

In an attempt to assuage the uncontrolled American fury which lashed out at all German artists, irrespective of the reservations held by many about Germany's unfortunate participation in the conflict, Friedberg announced through the press that he would give one-quarter of the receipts of his concert engagements during 1917-1918 to the American Red Cross. He said that aside from his desire to do something for the Red Cross, he believed that it offered an opportunity to express in some way his appreciation for the many courtesies extended to him in this country.

Although America declared war on Germany in April, 1917, following the sinking of the Lusitania, Friedberg appeared as soloist with the Philadelphia Orchestra, Leopold Stokowski, conductor, as late as the pair of concerts on October 19 and 20 of that year. He performed with them the works of two non-Germans, the E Flat Concerto of Liszt and the *Symphonic Variations* of César Franck. Afterwards he said that the attitude of both press and public "was wonderful."

As the international political situation became more critical Friedberg decided to make an attempt to secure a safe conduct permit to return to Germany. At first there seemed little hope, but through the help of Mme. Olga Samaroff Stokowski, who had an influential friend in Washington at that time, after months of uncertainty the safe conduct permit was granted on extremely short notice. The Friedbergs were to leave immediately on a small Norwegian steamer bound for Sweden.

It had been a difficult decision for the artist to make: to exchange a rich, comfortable country such as the United States, for war-torn Europe where the future looked dark. But Friedberg never regretted this step because he not only foresaw the difficulties of an alien in America, but he also realized the compromising position in which his kind friend, Frank Damrosch, would be placed if he attempted to retain a German teacher on the faculty of the Institute of Musical Art. Before leaving, Friedberg proposed to Damrosch that Ernest Hutcheson fill his post at the Institute. The suggestion was accepted.

On January 15, 1918, Carl and Gerda Friedberg, to the accompaniment of fond farewell wishes offered by their many friends, boarded the Bergensfjord to make the long journey back to Europe.

The ship called at Halifax, where it was inspected by the English authorities, and then proceeded on a long northern route to Norway. Since the steamer carried almost no cargo it pitched and rolled constantly so that, for the most part, the passengers were confined to their cabins. After a crossing in bitter weather that lasted three weeks, during which the ship passed through waters infested with many floating mines, the Friedbergs landed safely at Göteburg. Although a neutral country, Norway reflected the imprint of the war for there was no heat and food was very scarce; but this was only a sample of what awaited them in their own homeland. From Norway they passed through Sweden and Denmark and on to Germany, where they stopped for a short time with the mother of Gerda Friedberg.

Instead of the beautiful, prosperous country each had left, Germany now presented a pitiful, woebegone appearance. Food was scarce and very dear and, with little coal available, suffering was widespread. With the dwindling economic resources and social discontent which accompanied the growing realization that Germany might lose the war, the seeds of revolution had been sown. Violent disturbances became daily occurrences in the streets which now became no longer safe.

Before they left America, Mme. Stokowski had generously offered the Friedbergs the key to the Stokowski home in Munich. "Go and live in our house," she said, "if things get too bad at Düsseldorf." So the Friedbergs went to Munich, in southern Bavaria.

It was a very comfortable house, located near the River Isar on the outskirts of Munich, from which the Stokowskis themselves had hurriedly left when war broke out in 1914. Here the Friedbergs enjoyed as neighbors Bruno Walter, conductor of the Munich Opera, and Thomas Mann, the novelist.

At first Munich appeared to be a good place in which to live for there were better opportunities to procure food from the nearby farm country. Peasants came surreptitiously to the door to sell butter, flour, and eggs at enormous prices. Money had already begun to lose its value, for people were willing to pay almost any amount for food.

In spite of all the difficulties and hardships encountered

Friedberg, with much energy, began to resume his concert tours, playing in many of the German cities. His first appearances were in Munich, in 1919, where he gave two evenings devoted respectively to the works of Schumann, and of Brahms. Later, he appeared there in joint concert with his wife.

It was during this period that the artist first met Wilhelm Furtwängler, in the latter's first conducting post, at Lübeck, with whom he appeared as soloist in Beethoven's G Major (fourth) Concerto. Friedberg came home to Munich full of enthusiasm for the young conductor, convinced that Furtwängler would become one of the great figures in the musical world. In the following years they never missed an opportunity to perform together.

After the long hoped-for peace was finally established, the beaten, confused German army, without order, streamed back into the Fatherland. The soldiers, filled with disillusionment, presented a sad spectacle, their once smart uniforms in tatters, they on the verge of starvation.

The Peace Treaty itself left little hope of recovery for Germany for years to come. The internal situation rapidly deteriorated and soon a revolution by the masses was underway. Soldiers and marines took over the Government and the Kaiser fled to Holland. Citizens of means, including most of the aristocracy, were in danger of losing everything, for the Peoples' Government was unable to establish order. Bands of looters broke into houses and stores, occupied the castles and, inspired by a desire for revenge because of the hardships and suffering they had endured during the long war, took everything of value for their own use. The King of Bavaria fled. There was no police force, no telephone service, no public transportation. Stores dared not unlock their doors for fear of being looted.

At the height of the violence in Munich, Friedberg was away on a concert tour in East Germany from which all avenues of communication, for the time being, were severed.

Realizing that it was no longer safe to remain in the city, Gerda Friedberg decided to leave Munich. With all traffic immobilized, with even street cars at a standstill, she was forced to walk through the dark, unsafe streets to the railroad station, where she waited for hours for a train that would take her out of the city. A crowd stoned the train, and for many hours it was doubtful whether or not the so-called "Government" would permit it to leave the station.

After several days she arrived at Lake Constance near the Swiss border, where the situation was less critical, and attempted without success to communicate with her husband. Trains were still not operating and the news from Munich indicated that conditions there had worsened.

Finally, through her mother, Friedberg learned the whereabouts of his wife. It took him twenty-four hours, standing in a train packed with people, to join her at Lake Constance where they waited for conditions to improve.

After this frightening experience the Friedbergs decided to give up the Munich house and move to the Wätjen's family estate in the Harz Mountains. It was there that Gerda cherished the most beautiful memories of her childhood, for every year her family had spent the entire summer there. Now at last she could show her lovely home to her husband.

The large house was surrounded by a vast park, beyond which extended miles of woods and farm land. Here the two found the peace and quiet for which they had ardently longed. The estate was largely self-sustaining:—there were enough cattle to provide milk and butter; there were chickens and a large vegetable garden. Old farmers whose families had worked for the Wätjen family for generations did everything possible to make life comfortable and pleasant for them.

Sometimes gangs of soldiers from the cities came to the estate and carried away as much food as they could handle. No one dared object, for the men were hungry—and armed.

Here, at Altenrode, Friedberg completed his first edition

of the Beethoven sonatas, published by Schott in 1922. This edition differed markedly from others, many of which are so over-edited that it is difficult to determine where Beethoven left off and the editing began. In order to leave the original Beethoven version intact, Friedberg placed in parentheses all added dynamic, or expression marks. He also indicated approximate metronomic marks to establish the tempi of the various movements. The latter he changed, or added to in his second edition, published in 1927-28.

From this quiet, peaceful place Friedberg, never at rest, began to make plans for the coming season. Berlin was only six hours distant so he went there frequently to see his friends the Kreislers, the Fleschs, and the Schnabels.

Concert life began slowly to take form again and people longed for music more than ever. Such names as Schnabel, Busoni, d'Albert, Edwin Fischer, Backhaus, Frieda Kwast-Hodapp and many more appeared frequently in Berlin programs.

Friedberg renewed his friendship with Busoni who had left New York years before him. Busoni was happy to be back in his beloved Berlin, surrounded by his pupils and an intellectual group of admirers, of whom Friedberg was one. A recital by Busoni still was counted as one of the most interesting events in Berlin. After a visit to the capital, Friedberg always came back refreshed and stimulated.

There were other large cities such as Hanover near the estate where concert life was again taking shape. One day a manager telephoned Friedberg to ask him to come to Hanover in order to give his opinion of the talent of a youth of 18 who wished to go under his management. Friedberg went and was deeply impressed with the young man's ability. "Take him," he enthusiastically exclaimed, "by all means take him!" The young artist was Walter Gieseking, and in later years the two pianists often recalled with pleasure the circumstances surrounding their first meeting.

Although Friedberg had been absent four years, the

public had not forgotten him. With the improvement of the economic situation, recital engagements became more numerous so that with his Berlin appearance, in 1921, the artist re-established himself as one of the foremost German pianists.

Walter Niemann summed up the artistic stature of the pianist at this phase of his career in a chapter of his book, *Meister des Claviers*.

Within scarcely a decade, the King of the Rhenish pianists, Carl Friedberg, who makes his home in Munich, Berlin, or in the Harz Mountain estate, has taken his place in the first rank of German piano virtuosi. (. . .) One is so captivated by his eminent musicality that one is apt to forget his brilliant technique. He represents, in the best sense, the objective performer and is saved from th danger of academicism by his fiery Rhenish temperament, his Rhenish warmth and his typically Rhenish emotional spontaneity.

Despite his outstanding record as a teacher, he is a most unacademic, free, and impulsive artist. To begin with, everything he plays is well-defined, clear, and firmly stated. (. . .) He is an objective performer in the noblest sense of the word and a veritable artist who always 'steps back' in deference to the work he is playing, for he is never concerned with himself,—but solely with the task at hand. This explains the fact that this virtuoso, who is a match for the most prominent pianists, is equally well-known as a genuine, sensitive interpreter of chamber music. (. . .) Though his approach would justify terming him a 'classical' performer, it must be stated that he also masters all the attributes of 'modern' piano-style, thanks to his touch which is marvelous in its ability to convey the finest nuances and subtle shadings of a piano passage that, furthermore, even in forte passages, never becomes hard. Because of his deep musical

74

penetration, he has the exceptional capacity to create a definitive and exquisite musical sketch of every composition at the moment of its performance.

(. . .) He also possesses that rare mixture of Rhenish-South German temperament and an almost North-German inclination for intelligent musical analysis which is never obtrusive; the combination of these two factors permit him to make both a subjective and objective approach to his art.

In his erudition Friedberg far surpasses the usually narrow confines of his profession, with the result that he is elevated to the rank of sovereign master of the most varied classical, romantic and modern styles of the piano literature.[12]

When Artur Schnabel announced in the spring of 1920 that he was retiring as pianist of the Schnabel-Flesch-Becker Trio in order to devote himself exclusively to composing and to his own (solo) recitals, both violinist and cellist agreed that Friedberg was the only possible successor to Schnabel.

Carl Flesch has said that "Friedberg was equal to Schnabel in his musical and technical gifts, but as a personality, he was completely different." Continuing, he wrote:

(. . .) [Friedberg's] fine-nerved, subtle, natural and unaffected temperament, poetic in the best sense of the word, (. . .) allowed him to communicate to the listener the intimate mood of a work, undamaged by intellectual dissection. At such moments his features acquired a spiritual expression which made him appear almost beautiful. He somewhat resembled Voltaire and had a slight lisp.[13]

Friedberg served as the pianist member of the trio, with Flesch and Becker, until 1922. In assuming the pianistic duties of this ensemble, his first regular post since he terminated his activities with the Frankfurter Trio twelve years before, the artist was again able to gratify his urge to perform through his favorite avenue of music-making. He regarded chamber music literature the highest form of musical expression through which such composers as Mozart, Beethoven, Schumann, Brahms, César Franck and others had attained their loftiest heights.

Meanwhile, the German political situation continued precariously. Millions of unemployed walked the roads, traveling from city to city in search of work, sleeping on hay in barns or in open fields, begging food from door to door.

A strong influx of Communism from Russia brought added economic complications and, with inflation, the value of stocks dwindled. The mark depreciated to the point that a pound of butter cost 1,000,000 marks. Once Friedberg returned from a concert tour with his suitcase filled with paper money, equal to the price of a dozen eggs.

A new military organization was formed, "The Steel Helmets," consisting of the sons of former army officers which attempted to take over the Government in order to suppress the spread of Communism.

Frequently, after dark, a state of siege would be declared within a city, and all persons were ordered off the streets. Evening concerts and theatrical performances were cancelled. Also, since trains never arrived or left on schedule, concertizing was made difficult, almost impossible.

An interesting personality Friedberg met in Berlin was Professor Leo Kestenberg, a highly cultured man, and *Kultusminister* in Germany. Kestenberg was much impressed with the pianist's art and musical ideals, and the two men often met to discuss artistic problems.

At this time Franz Schreker, one of the outstanding composers of the very early Twenties, was appointed Director of the Berlin State Hochschule for Music. Both

Plate 6

Carl Friedberg with his Master-Class at the Cologne Conservatory, 1913

Plate 7

Carl Friedberg is soloist at the Bonn Beethoven Festival, 1914

Schreker and Kestenberg attempted to persuade Friedberg to head the piano department at the Hochschule. The artist was in the midst of considering the offer when Frank Damrosch, his wife and daughter, arrived from America for a visit with the Friedbergs. Damrosch had come to Europe with the express purpose of persuading Friedberg to return to his teaching post at the Institute of Musical Art.

Friedberg was confronted with a difficult decision. He had renewed the roots of his career in his homeland. To return to America would mean to decline the post at the Hochschule. Taking into consideration the German political and financial situation, he agreed to Damrosch's request that he return to New York in January, 1923, to conduct a Master Class for a period of ten weeks. That this was a wise decision was proved in the years to come.

Two letters written to Friedberg at this time have been preserved, one from d'Albert, the other from Emile R. Blanchet, the Swiss-French composer. d'Albert's letter, dated simply "May, 1921," brought news that he had performed his new trio with Berber, violinist, and Hegar, cellist. Although the audience had reacted favorably to the work, letters the composer had received from certain of his colleagues afterward, made him think that "the piece is not very interesting." d'Albert also mentioned another piano concerto that he had sent to his publisher and said that as soon as there were copies available he would send one to Friedberg. "You spoke of wanting a new work to perform," he wrote, "so I can provide you with this shortly, from Schott."

Blanchet's letter, dated May 1, 1921, thanked the pianist for performing his works and told of some recent compositions:

Dear Mr. Friedberg:
  I was greatly pleased to hear quite some time ago that you had added some of my Preludes to your reper-

toire and that you played them at your concerts. All my efforts to get hold of your address were without success until finally Mrs. von Kresz Drewett suggested that I inquire about it at the Link Management. Although belatedly, I want you to know that I consider it a great honor for my works to be performed by a Master of your rank. I could not find out which of the Preludes you have been playing and I would appreciate your letting me know, if you can find the time to do so. Also I would like to know which of my compositions you own. Since the Preludes, I have written many works which seem to me to be of greater importance. Do you have the 'Dix Etudes nouvelles' and the 'Neuf Etudes de Concert'? I would be very glad to send you all those you do not yet have.

    I remain very sincerely yours,

        E. R. Blanchet

In January, 1923, Carl and Gerda Friedberg returned to New York for a two-and-a-half months' stay, stopping at the San Remo Hotel on Central Park West. At this time the pianist played only two solo recitals, both in the Recital Hall of the Institute. With Sascha Jacobson, violinist, and Willem Willeke, cellist, he also gave two chamber music concerts.

With the success of the Master Class, which was attended by a large group of performers and listeners, Friedberg was re-appointed a regular member of the faculty, occupying the post as Head Teacher of the Pianoforte at the Institute of Musical Art for the next 23 years.

V

THE JULLIARD SCHOOL YEARS

(1923-1946)

On the completion of his brief Master Class at the Institute of Musical Art Carl Friedberg with his wife returned to the Harz Mountain home for several months and, thereafter, each summer until they moved to Baden in 1924. Because of the critical state of German economy there was still no concert life to speak of, and the activities of the Friedberg-Flesch-Becker Trio ceased temporarily. However, the pianist made a tour of Holland in the summer—his first since the war—performing also in both Switzerland and England. Because of illness he was unable to fulfill all his English engagements. (This very probably was the first indication of the grave illness that soon followed).

The season 1923-1924 marked the trek of many European artists back to the United States to resume careers cut short by the war. It also saw the debuts of many new ones. Within six days in New York City seven pianists were heard: Rachmaninoff, Friedberg, Levitzki, Grainger, Gabrilowitsch, Elly Ney and Katherine Bacon.

The German repertory was gradually reinstated at the Metropolitan, which added such new singers as Rethberg, Jeritza, Curt Taucher, Schützendorf and Schorr, while many others returned to resume the roles they had performed at that theater prior to 1918.

Besides the large number of instrumentalists and singers many noted European conductors also came, either as permanent or guest conductors of the old and new orchestras, a number of which had steadily increased after the war. During the 1920's the leading conductors, many of whom were German, were Artur Bodansky, Bruno Walter, Fritz Busch, Otto Klemperer, Wilhelm Furtwängler, Willem Mengelberg, Serge Koussevitzky, Leopold Stokowski, Walter Damrosch, Fritz Reiner, Frederick Stock, Pierre Monteux, and Arturo Toscanini. With this galaxy of artists and conductors the American public developed a wider interest in concert-going than formerly.

Recovering from his indisposition in England, Friedberg returned alone to New York in the fall of 1923 to teach. His wife remained temporarily in Europe to superintend the move into the new house they had recently bought at Baden Baden. With Bodansky conducting, Friedberg was soloist at the November concert of the Friends of Music and was acclaimed for his "genuinely beautiful" performance of the Mendelssohn G minor Concerto. In December, at Aeolian Hall, he gave a recital devoted to works of Brahms and Schumann.

Stating that this was Friedberg's first recital in New York in seven years, the *Sun* commented that ". . . before the evening closed, it looked as if every pianist of note had come to listen and to learn." [1] The critic observed that the artist had grown in musical stature since his last New York appearance and proclaimed his musicianship "superb." The pianist was heard in a second recital devoted entirely to the music of Chopin on January 21.

Subsequently, Friedberg, as one of eighteen pianists performed in a benefit concert given at the Metropolitan Opera House for the aged composer-pianist Moritz Moszkowski, then living in Paris in destitute circumstances. Seated at the other seventeen pianos were Myra Hess, Ossip Gabrilowitsch, Sigismund Stojowski, Alexander Siloti, Elly Ney, Ernest

Schelling, Ernest Hutcheson, Harold Bauer, Mischa Levitzki, Alexander Brailowsky, Josef Lhévinne, Guy Maier, Yolanda Mero, Ethel Leginska, Guiomar Novaes, Germaine Schnitzer, and Lee Pattison. The pianists performed singly, in duos, trios and the concert ended with the "March" from Schumann's *Carnaval,* which made a splendid finale with eighteen pianists under the leadership of Walter Damrosch.

Following an appearance at the Beethoven Association as assisting artist with a quartet led by Carl Flesch, Friedberg left for a mid-western tour, during which he was to have performed for the first time as soloist with Gabrilowitsch and the Detroit Symphony.

However, in the middle of his tour, after having performed with the Chicago Symphony in late January 1924, the pianist was suddenly seized with a raging fever accompanied by swelling of his hands. Cancelling the remainder of his concerts, Friedberg returned to his apartment at the Great Northern Hotel in New York. There his doctor diagnosed the malady as rheumatic fever and wished to send him to the hospital; but the pianist stubbornly insisted on treatment at his hotel.

On being informed of her husband's illness, his wife soon arrived from Europe to find him seriously ill, his hands bandaged and his vitality extremely low.

In spite of his illness, Friedberg's first thought was of his pupils. He ordered a piano moved into the apartment and send word to them to come and play for him. Unable for the first time in his life to illustrate at the piano, he proceeded forthwith to teach from his bed, this despite his doctor's warning that excessive movement, or nervous excitement would affect his heart. Assuredly his recovery would have been hastened had he not undertaken this strenuous convalescence, but he well knew that without his guidance his pupils' progress would suffer. Not only did he give lessons in his sickroom, but from there he also planned two successful recitals given by his pupils at the Institute.

Regrettably his insistence on teaching marked the beginning of a serious heart condition from which he was never thereafter completely free.

Confined to bed for three months, Friedberg suffered not only great physical pain but also extreme mental torture that he might not ever be able to play again. Although his left hand was less afflicted and soon appeared normal, his right hand was completely paralysed—he was unable to open his fingers.

During this critical hour of his career the invalid received many visitors including the conductor, Furtwängler. Together they read the score of Stravinsky's "Le Sacre du Printemps," then having had its first performance in New York by Monteux and the Boston Symphony. Mischa Elman also delighted him when he brought his recording of the Schubert-Friedberg "Rondo in D Major." But perhaps the person who helped him most was Gabrilowitsch, who came frequently to see him and who always said upon leaving: "You *will* regain the use of your right hand and you *will* perform with me in Detroit!"

In March Carl and Gerda Friedberg moved to the San Remo Hotel so as to be near Central Park in which he began to take daily short, slow walks. By May he was well enough to sail for Europe.

How fortunate that they had chosen Baden Baden as their new home! At this noted spa Friedberg was able to secure the finest care for his hands. With great patience he underwent the necessary treatments. Each day his fingers were stretched and massaged. Although this phase of his recovery strained to the limit his sensitive nervous system, outwardly he remained calm and controlled. His will to overcome the disaster and regain use of his fingers was maintained and directed by his one constant thought: "I *must* play again." He devised various exercises to strengthen and gain control of his fingers. Many pupils came to see him at 11 Werderstrasse and played for him there. The summer was particularly beautiful with cooling breezes from the near-by mountains, and with many days of bright sunlight, together with myriads of flowers, all of which helped to bring about a virtually complete cure. What Gabrilowitsch had confidently said to him months before now began to come true.

Baden Baden, one of the most delightful smaller cities in Germany, through which flows the little River Oos, situated on the edge of the Black Forest, proved to be an ideal summer residence. Here Nature in all her beauty combined with the city's old cultural background to offer many opportunities for serious music-making. The house where Brahms had lived is still in existence as is the Hotel Bären where Clara Schumann was frequently a guest. In addition to the Kurhaus and Kur Gardens, where orchestral concerts were (and are) presented daily during the summer, there is the Kleines Theater, a charming French-style structure originally built for Berlioz.

Inspired by Friedberg's choice of residence, Carl Flesch now moved from Berlin to Baden and the Trio, in which Felix Salmond replaced Becker as cellist (for only one year) made plans to present a chamber music festival in September of each year in the Kleines Theater.

Friedberg returned to New York in the fall and performed the Beethoven E flat ("Emperor") Concerto with Gabrilowitsch in Detroit under the greatest difficulty. Happily the audience was not aware of this and gave both pianist and conductor a tremendous ovation at the end of the concerto.

This experience enabled Friedberg to regain belief in himself as a pianist, although he sensed he was not ready to undertake a recital. He contented himself with playing chamber music, in America and abroad, occasionally venturing one or two solos.

In 1924 the Juilliard Graduate School, with Dr. Eugene Noble as Secretary of the Juilliard Foundation, opened its doors for instruction in the former Vanderbilt residence on East Fifty-Second Street in midtown New York. Among the pianists engaged as teachers were Carl Friedberg,* James Friskin, Ernest Hutcheson, Josef and Rosina Lhévinne, Olga Samaroff and Alexander Siloti. The vocal teachers were Marcella Sembrich, Florence Page Kimball, Anna Schön-René, Paul Reimers and Francis Rogers. Leopold Auer, Paul Kochanski, Hans Letz and Edouard Dethier were appointed teachers of violin. Rubin Goldmark taught composition, and Felix Salmond, cello.

Friedberg unsuccessfully tried to persuade Dr. Noble to locate the Juilliard School outside of New York, in White Plains, or in some other near-by suburban town, for the reason that study and natural living would be less tense and less expensive than in a large city.

The pianist now made the Gladstone Hotel, situated a short distance down the street from Juilliard, his musical headquarters and traveled uptown two days a week for his teaching at the Institute of Musical Art.

Stravinsky also resided at the Gladstone and Friedberg received the composer in his comfortable suite with two Steinway pianos, a grand and an upright, where he taught his private class. Many of his pupils played Stravinsky's works in this studio and received valuable suggestions from the composer.

The artist-teacher now established a pattern which enabled him to devote approximately seven months of the year to a heavy teaching schedule at the Institute of Musical Art and the Juilliard School, interspersed with brief concert-tours. He returned to Europe for the summer and early

---

* At first Frank Damrosch was opposed to Friedberg's joining the Juilliard faculty, but after it was decided to merge the Institute with the Juilliard Foundation (with the former designated as the Under-Graduate School and the Juilliard as the Graduate School), Damrosch gave his consent,—provided Friedberg retained his position at the Institute.

84

fall months, when he had the leisure to make more extended concert tours and to perform chamber music.

Among the friends whom the artist and his wife saw during these years were Joseph Szigeti, who had resided at the San Remo when the Friedbergs lived there; the Artur Schnabels, to whose home they often went to hear Schnabel play his own compositions and discuss his works with his colleague; and Myra Hess, who came for her first American tour in 1922 under the management of his sister, Annie Friedberg. For Dame Myra, Friedberg always had the greatest admiration and respect. Their warm friendship which lasted to the end of his days was a source of mutual joy and inspiration.

In 1927 John Erskine became the first president of Juilliard and three years later the school moved uptown to its new building on Claremont Avenue adjoining the Institute of Musical Art, near Columbia University. Erskine retired in 1937 and Ernest Hutcheson then became president. Supported by the income derived from a fourteen million dollars endowment, entrance to the graduate school was solely by means of fellowships awarded through qualifying examinations.* With a faculty of the highest rank the School attracted young musicians from the United States, Canada and later Europe, becoming, between the years 1925-1945, one of the renowned musical institutions of the world.

Meanwhile Baden Baden had become a music center, developing around the two great teachers, Friedberg and Flesch. Many of his Juilliard students, loathe to interrupt their study, followed Friedberg to Germany every summer. Chamber music concerts were resumed by Friedberg, Flesch and Piatigorsky, who replaced Salmond as cellist. The com-

* The Foundation Library Center records the original endowment of the Juilliard Musical Foundation at $13,460,508 dollars, giving as its reference Kiger's *Operating Principles of the Larger Foundations,* page 124.

bination of concerts with teaching continued a number of years in that beautiful spot, and proved stimulating to all.

Always interested in new music, Friedberg joined with Szigeti, in 1923, to give the premiere performance of Ernest Bloch's Sonata for Violin and Piano * at the first festival of the International Society for Contemporary Music at Salzburg. At the Baden Baden contemporary festivals he heard the first performances of Kurt Weill's *Aufstieg und Fall der Stadt Mahagonny* (Rise and Fall of the City of Mahagonny) and *Die Dreigroschenoper* (The Threepenny Opera). One of his most vivid memories of these festivals was Rudolf Serkin's performance of piano compositions by Hindemith, the young pianist creating a wonderful impression with his remarkable talent and brilliant command of the instrument. At various European festivals he met the composers Ravel, Milhaud, Prokofieff and Schönberg.

Friedberg's friendship with the violinist, Erika Morini, and the pianist, Vladimir Horowitz, stemmed from these years too. Both were frequent visitors to Baden Baden and guests of Carl Flesch during several festivals.

Booked by his manager for a large European tour— January to April, 1927—and unwilling to leave his pupils for so long a time without a teacher, Friedberg arranged for Lonny Epstein, teacher at the Cologne Conservatory, to take over his class at the Institute of Musical Art.

In the fall of 1928 he made his first tour of the American West Coast. In addition to performing in numerous smaller cities, Friedberg was heard in Portland, Seattle, Los Angeles, Santa Barbara, and San Francisco, in which latter city he played the Brahms B flat Concerto (the first time that work had ever been given in San Francisco) with Alfred Hertz, conductor, achieving one of the greatest artistic triumphs of his entire career. In all, he was hailed as one of the greatest pianists of his time.

* Friedberg also performed this work with Rudolf Polk, violinist, in 1924, in New York.

86

The artist had not given a New York recital for five years and in that same season announced that his program, in addition to the classics, would contain new works by Blanchet, Toch, Milhaud, and Rachmaninoff. At the last moment, to the disappoinment of many, he was persuaded by his sister-manager to replace the modern works with classical pieces for which he was already famous. However, he played these contemporary works along with pieces by Prokofieff and Debussy in Boston, Buffalo, Baltimore, Washington and other cities.

After Lonny Epstein was appointed to the faculty of the Institute of Musical Art, Friedberg, for several seasons, went twice a year to Europe to play concerts, both in the summer and again during the Christmas Holidays.

His summer activities in Europe were extensive and he gave twelve concerts within five weeks before crowded houses and enthusiastic critics. At Frankfurt-am-Main he performed the Liszt E flat Concerto in the Fiftieth Anniversary celebrations of the Hoch'sche Conservatorium, and gave recitals in Vienna and Brussels, in the latter city his first appearance since the war. He also performed with the State Opera Orchestra in Dresden under Fritz Busch, the Königsberg Orchestra under Herman Scherchen, the Berlin Opera Orchestra with Otto Klemperer, and conducted the Baden-Baden orchestra in an all-Brahms concert.

One of the exotic personalities the pianist encountered during that time was Rabindranath Tagore whom he met at Darmstadt at the residence of the former Duke von Hessen, where the Bengalese poet lectured on Eastern Philosophy and read some of his poetry. Afterwards, in conversation with Friedberg, Tagore commented that Bach was the only Western composer whose works were appreciated in India. This was true, he said, because of Bach's contrapuntal style, in which the linear lines are followed and understood by East Indian audiences. On the other hand, he added, his people are quite unable to fathom homophonic music.

Another of his long-remembered European experiences took place in July, 1930, when Friedberg attended the Wagner Festival at Bayreuth. There he heard *Tristan und Isolde,* conducted by Toscanini, and *Parsifal,* conducted by Dr. Karl Muck, both performances he termed "outstandingly beautiful."

The economic crash of 1929 did not materially affect the artist for he had his two lucrative teaching posts, as well as a large class of private pupils. Nevertheless, as did every concert artist, he found fewer concert engagements, with many orchestras unable to continue. Since the depression was world-wide, musical conditions in Europe were the same. With the invention of the sound picture, theater musicians were deprived of the means of earning a livelihood, while the development of radio offered the opportunity to reach greater audiences, though untrained for listening to serious music.

Interestingly, Carl Friedberg inaugurated the first NBC radio network program devoted to the performance of great music, on January 10, 1931. He played works by Brahms, Prokofieff and Chopin. In February he appeared with the "Dollar Symphony," conducted by Erno Rapeé at the Roxy Theater as soloist in the Schumann concerto, which was broadcast throughout the country and by short-wave to England and Germany. Other New York orchestral appearances were with the American Orchestral Society, Chalmers Clifton, conductor, with whom he played the Brahms B flat Concerto; the Philharmonic Young People's Concerts, playing the Franck *Symphonic Variations* under Ernest Schelling; and the National Orchestral Association, conducted by Leon Barzin, with which group he appeared on two occasions, playing the Schumann concerto at the Association's opening concert in 1930 and, later, the Beethoven "Emperor" Concerto.

The summer of 1932 was the last year the Friedberg-Flesch-Piatigorsky Trio performed together in Baden Baden.

With political tension in Germany, concert halls were half empty. In Freiburg, where the trio gave a concert, only a few attended. During intermission time, the artists asked, "What happened to the audience?" "They all went outside to the *Sportplatz* to listen to some crazy man." The "crazy man" was Hitler.

Among outstanding concerts presented by this famous Trio was that of September 8, 1930 in Baden Baden. Each artist performed a concerto in the *Grosse Bühne,* Ernst Mehlich, conductor. Piatigorsky played Haydn's D Major cello Concerto; Flesch, the Bruch G minor; and Friedberg the Schumann Concerto. For several years these concerts had played an important part in the musical life of Germany; for they were broadcast on a national network.

Although Friedberg planned to give a number of concerts in celebration of the One Hundredth Anniversary of the birth of Brahms, most were cancelled, for with Hitler in power, it was no longer possible for anyone of Jewish origin to concertize in Germany. However, as late as December, 1932, Carl Friedberg returned to make concert appearances in Holland and a few cities in Germany, opening his tour in Amsterdam at the Christmas Day matinee of the Concert-gebouw, Mengelberg, conductor. One of his last German concerts took place in January, 1933, at Aachen, with the Städtische Orchestra, Dr. Peter Raabe, conductor, when the pianist performed the Brahms B flat Concerto.

Among the truly great performances of his career must be mentioned two concerts with the New York Philharmonic-Symphony, Bruno Walter, conductor, on November 23 and 24 of the same year, at which time the pianist performed the same work, concerning which Olin Downes wrote:

> Mr. Friedberg played the formidable part of the Brahms concerto with admirable breadth and energy, which if anything out-Brahmsed Brahms. It is, however,

probable that Brahms himself played the B flat concerto that way—immense pawsfull of notes, immense breadth and fire, and the piano a second orchestra. Mr. Friedberg's vigorous rhythms and attacks had their due contrast in the treatment of the lyrical phrases. All details contributed to the big lines of the structure and, above all, to the sensation of the grandeur of great spaces. This was maintained in the 'demoniac' scherzo, but the slow movement was playing of another kind, playing which matched the poetry of the musical thought. In short, it was a performance by a pianist who knew the grand manner and whose traditions are particularly of the period that saw the culmination of Brahms's creative career. Mr. Friedberg was worthily applauded, and so was the Brahms concerto! [2]

In 1933 the Friedbergs decided to sell their house in Baden Baden and go, instead, to Ascona, Switzerland, to the Hotel Monte Verita. During this summer they attended the stimulating lectures given by the *Eranos Tagung,* an international organization devoted to a better understanding of religion and philosophy in both Eastern and Western civilizations. Among the interesting speakers heard were Martin Buber, Heinrich Zimmer and Dr. C. G. Jung.

The following summer the Friedbergs took a house in Ascona, overlooking Lago Maggiore. With one exception (1936) this remained their summer residence for the next five years and his pupils came as they had formerly come to Baden.

During these and succeeding years New York provided a rich musical fare which included concerts by well-known artists as well as debut recitals by many young talents. It also marked the first visits to the United States by several of Europe's leading contemporary composers.

The debuts of Menuhin as a boy of eleven and that of the young Horowitz evoked considerable enthusiasm in

Friedberg. (Menuhin's younger sister, Yaltah, later studied privately with the pianist.) He was also greatly interested in the New York appearances of Ravel, Prokofieff, and Schönberg, all of whom performed or conducted their own works. He attended many of the concerts given by the League of Composers and was present at the American premiere of such significant stage works as Grünberg's *Emperor Jones,* Thomson's *Four Saints in Three Acts,* and Shostakovitch's *Lady Macbeth of Mzensk,* to mention a few. He also followed the Broadway stage, enjoying such productions as Gershwin's *Porgy and Bess* (original opera version), *Kykunkor* (African Ballet-Opera), and the musical shows of Weill, Rodgers and Hammerstein, and others. For unusual concerts or stage productions he always bought extra tickets which he distributed to deserving pupils who he thought should have the opportunity to hear such works.

In January 1934, in his sixty-second year, Friedberg gave a New York recital at Town Hall which will be long remembered for its excellence. The program comprised works by Schumann ("Two Romances," "Intermezzo," and the *Etudes Symphoniques),* Beethoven *(Sonta Op.* 81a), a Brahms group which included Book II of the *Paganini Variations,* and a Chopin group. Howard Taubman wrote that "the recital was distinguished by an authenticity and rectitude of style, brilliance of technic and breath and profundity of insight that must be the despair of younger and ambitious artists."

Stating that the pianist would probably be categorized as belonging to the "old school," Taubman said: "Old school or new school, his playing has the temperament and fire of youth, the clarity and perception of maturity. The audience seemed to be aware of these things; the applause was spontaneous and prolonged. Whatever Mr. Friedberg's background may be, he is, on the basis of last night's interpretations, a pianist with a future." [3]

In the fall the artist made his first appearance at the

Worcester Festival, Albert Stoessel, conductor, performing the Beethoven C minor Concerto, for which he was given an ovation. Prior to the concert he gave an interview to a local newspaper, in which he reminded the reader that the responsibility of the success of a concert is not alone that of the performers: "The layman should come to a concert more prepared," Friedberg said. "Laymen should learn more of the technical side of music, through reading and by experience. An appreciation of the subtleties of the music will add to the enjoyment of the program. Even people without 'an ear for music' can learn to distinguish the finer points and enjoy the music fully." [4]

In the spring of 1935 the pianist appeared as soloist in one of the series given at the Juilliard School devoted to "The Literature of the Concerto," playing the Beethoven C Minor Concerto. Although Albert Stoessel was the regular conductor of the orchestra, both Friedberg and Ernest Hutcheson conducted concertos performed by other faculty pianists.

Now that Germany was closed to him Friedberg's orchestral appearances (as those of many other artists) became fewer, and confined for the most part to the United States and Canada. Among the orchestras with which he performed are the Cincinnati Symphony (Goossens); Toronto (Sir Ernest MacMillan); Montreal; Syracuse; Reading, Pennsylvania (Hans Kindler); New York Federal Symphony Orchestra, (Chalmers Clifton); Toledo (Hans Lange). On February 8, 1938, Friedberg played at The White House for President and Mrs. Roosevelt.

The pianist continued with his chamber music activities, presenting with Enesco the latter's second *Sonata for Violin and Piano* at the Beethoven Association. Later, for the same organization, he appeared with Gaspar Cassadó, Spanish cellist, with whom he performed Beethoven's cello *Sonata in A Major Op.* 69. Afterwards Cassadó wrote a note of appreciation to his distinguished colleague:

92

9, Feb. 1937

Maestro:

Having played with you, means for me not only a real pleasure, but it is like a confession, a dialogue with the great artist and the great Master that you are—the music and you, this is complete unity: that is the secret—

I thank you with all my heart for the opportunity to play with you and I remain with the expression of my most sincere admiration,

Yours,

Gaspar Cassadó

Friedberg spent the summer of 1936 in La Jolla, California, where he taught during July and August. This western small city was hardly an adequate substitute for his beloved Europe and in a letter to Lonny Epstein, dated July 20, he expressed his dissatisfaction at the turn the world had begun to take:

> . . . Besides I don't feel very well 'spiritually.' By some occult powers within myself I am aware of looming disaster. The unrest in the world and especially the discontent are too prominent and should it happen again that sheer force will be established as the normal condition, that will be the end of everything treasured and dear to me.

Another letter to his devoted colleague, dated August 15, found him in brighter spirits: "I had lunch today with Klemperer . . . then paid a call to the Schönbergs."

He returned to New York by way of Texas where he attended the Texas Centennial Celebration in Dallas and celebrated his sixty-fourth birthday with several of his former students resident there. He also planned a fall appearance with his old friend Paul van Katjwick, conductor of the Dallas Symphony.

In 1937, with Daniil Karpilowsky, violinist, and Felix

Salmond, cellist, Friedberg formed the Trio of New York, giving with them a series of concerts at the Mannes School during the first season, followed by a series of five concerts at Town Hall during 1938-1939. In December of the latter year the Trio gave a memorable New Friends of Music evening at Carnegie Hall, an all-Brahms concert. For several seasons these artists were a valued and highly respected asset to New York's musical life. The Trio of New York toured the United States and Canada, but disbanded when Karpilowsky went to California to live.

The summers of 1937 and 1938 found the Friedbergs back in Ascona. However, in 1938 his teaching was cut short by a war scare and they hurried home to America. It was then Carl Friedberg became a citizen of the United States. The following summer, after the international scene had quieted, the two went to Sweden, to a little town near Stockholm, for a month's rest. After three weeks another war scare sent them home. This time the scare was real, for Hitler had invaded Poland. On the journey home, in the middle of the ocean, they heard that England had declared war on Germany.

During World War II Friedberg taught for one summer at Blue Hill, Maine, occupying the Kneisel cottage and having for neighbors his friends the Kreislers. The next four summers he took a house on Nantucket Island where his pupils now came. With the gasoline shortage everyone went about on foot or rode bicycles, which contributed to the quietness and restfulness essential to the artist's well-being. Here war seemed quite remote—until news of the Hiroshima bomb.

One of Friedberg's last important chamber music appearances in New York occurred in February, 1944, where at Town Hall he performed as assisting artist with the Roth Quartet in the Brahms Piano Quintet in F minor.

He was not only interested in playing chamber music

94

himself but greatly interested in the performances of other artists in this medium. He particularly admired the Adolf Busch-Rudolf Serkin sonata-duo, whose concerts he attended and whose broadcasts he followed, as a note from Busch dated November 3, 1944, suggests:

Dear Mr. Friedberg;
Thank you so much for your note. How kind of you, to take the trouble. But it was a great pleasure for me (also for Serkin) to know that you listened in and liked it. There is nothing more rewarding for a musician than to be praised by a fellow-musician whom one holds in such high esteem as I have held you since my early youth.
Thank you ever so much once more and kindest regards to you and Mrs. Friedberg.
Yours,
Adolf Busch

The pianist's last New York recital "down-town" took place at Hunter College Auditorium in 1945, when he played works by Brahms, Beethoven, Schumann and Chopin. He drew a large and responsive audience. A few days after the concert Felix Salmond, the cellist, wrote him as follows:

My dear Carl—
I am still under the spell of your truly exquisite and touching performance on Friday past. As you well know, Mozart gave his highest praise to the performer who could 'play in the proper tempo, give expression to every note, appoggiatura, etc., tastefully and as they are written, so as to create the impression that the player had *composed* the piece.' Most assuredly he would have delighted in your masterly, poetic playing of your whole programme on Friday last. It was full of true nobility of feeling and understanding; subtle and at the same time

95

simple, as all great playing is. Also it had the quality which only a lifetime of devotion to and experience of the greatest of the Arts can bring to an audience.

I have heard much great music-making and treasure each experience. Your playing on Friday will always remain one of my happiest and most vivid memories. It must have been an inspiration and a *lesson* to the *young* pianists in your audience as well as to all your colleagues who rejoiced in your triumph.

Your old friend and admirer

Felix

From 1923-1946, both at Juilliard and in his studio Friedberg developed pianists whose achievements are impressive, many of them having made successful European as well as American tours, with others occupying prominent teaching positions at leading college and university schools of music over the country. Among the outstanding are William Masselos, Maro Ajemian, Vivian Rivkin, Marienka Michna, Catherine Carver Burton, and Jane Carlson, all now well-known recitalists. One of the younger pianists steadily gaining fame is Malcolm Frager whose only teacher was Carl Friedberg with whom he studied privately from 1949-1955. Following winning the Leventritt Award in 1959 and the Queen Elizabeth of Belgium Prize in 1960, young Frager made his debut with the New York Philharmonic Symphony, Bernstein conductor, in May 1959, followed by appearances as soloist with leading American orchestras and a tour of our cities. His first European tour was in the fall of 1961.

Friedberg also developed several excellent two-piano teams of which Appleton and Field, and Ferrante and Teicher are the most prominent. Among former students who have made careers as accompanying artists are Anthony Kooiker, who toured with Albert Spalding for several years, and Sergius Kagen, teacher of vocal literature and accompanying at Juilliard.

Among the noted musicians who visited the artist-teacher's classes at the Juilliard School was Vladimir Dukelsky, composer, who set down the impression of his visit in a letter dated February 9, 1946:

Dear Mr. Friedberg,

My visit to your studios at Juilliard yesterday was an unforgettable experience. You are the only great pedagogue I know of who busies himself not with merely *how* to play, but above all *what* to play. As a rule, so-called 'Master Teachers' (?) inflict the same shop-worn repertoire on their pupils and make them vie with one another in performing the same; you lay stress not only on finished execution—of which your pupils gave magnificent proof—but first and last, musical awareness. By this I mean not only good taste and correct style, but being attuned to what goes on in the creative musical world. Contemporary composers owe you a great debt for such a refreshing and truly youthful point of view; so many of them, including the writer, complain of lack of co-operation on the interpreter's part.

The little dark girl who played first—the one with the extra-small hands—was one of the most immaculate technicians I've ever heard, but she was also a thoroughly sound musician. Should she give a recital, I shall most certainly be there. As to Miss Therrien, I repeat that with earnest study and perseverance she may become the first really *good female composer*. I wish you would tell Miss Therrien that with her talent it would be a dire shame were she to give up composition and passively subscribe to the fashionable theory that there is no such animal as an important woman composer. Why not attempt to prove that such an animal in fact exists in her own person? Tell her to remember that competition in the virtuoso field is fast and furious, but the composer's market for women is wide open.

I heard Miss Carlson in the piano part of the Hindemith work several weeks back, and marveled at her distinguished and thoroughly mature performance. I am only sorry that she bothered to learn the very unworthy Rachmaninoff piece, which outside of its lack of musical worth did not seem to suit her talents. She is already a superb artist and I spoke to her on a previous occasion of joining me in a venture which I call "The Society for Forgotten Music." I am suddenly struck with the idea that you might be fascinated by this plan because, from the brief conversation we had, you are obviously just as much at home with the minor gods, doomed to oblivion, as with similar composers of today, whose lot may well be the same after their death. . . .

Sincerely,
Vladimir Dukelsky

In addition to his piano-teaching Friedberg also taught ensemble classes at Juilliard; admittance was eagerly sought by not only his own students but also by those of other teachers. Among numerous instrumentalists who gained much from his authoritative command of the chamber music repertoire may be mentioned the composer-pianist, Paul Nordoff (pupil of Goldmark and Samaroff), in whose compositions Friedberg was much interested, and the cellist, Leonard Rose (pupil of Salmond).

Sergius Kagen, one of Friedberg's young Russian students at Juilliard in the late 1920's and early 1930's has given us considerable insight into the artist's role as teacher. His article, written for inclusion here, is entitled:

THE TEACHING OF CARL FRIEDBERG

"Teaching certain aspects of music, especially teaching the performance of music, does not lend itself too well to a description in writing, beyond the barest essentials of elementary techniques. The impact upon the student of the teacher's personality, culture, talent, taste and, consequently, of his approach to the music and the instrument, is immeasurably more potent than any words he may use in his teaching. What he says may even become nearly unintelligible, if separated from the interplay of the two personalities and of the music which has brought them together. It is, perhaps, because of this vast gulf between the verbal means at the teacher's disposal and his total artistic and musical personality, that so very few books and articles dealing with musical performance and interpretation ever succeed in conveying the real significance of his artistic aims and of the means he employs to attain them.

"I would, therefore, prefer not to try to put down Carl Friedberg's words about music and pianism that I still remember and that may mean so much to me personally. I would much rather write of him as of a great artist whose influence contributed so much to my own development as a musician and as a pianist.

"I first decided that I had to study with Carl Friedberg when I heard him play the Beethoven C minor Concerto with the New York Philharmonic. I believe, though I am not certain, that the conductor was Willem Mengelberg.* I have no recollection whatsoever of the rest of the program. The only thing I remember in detail, even now, some thirty years later, is Carl Friedberg's playing. It was utterly extraordinary in one particular detail: the instrument seemed to speak. The rhythm, inflexion and articulation of every phrase were so remarkably natural, free of any effort and so utterly unselfconscious that his playing seemed somehow to create an illusion of transcending the limitations of a percussion instrument, which even a modern pianoforte still is basically. I have heard many pianists play more brilliantly, more dazzlingly, play louder or softer or faster or more

* Note: If by Mengelberg, this concert took place on December 3, 1926.

50401

learnedly. I have never before or since heard any pianist match completely the extraordinary ability that Carl Friedberg possessed to shape a musical phrase into something so naturally rhythmical, effortless, unostentatious, and therefore so eloquent, that the playing reminded one more of human speech, with its inexhaustible variety of inflexion, than of any musical instrument, or even of singing.

"As I studied with him I gradually became more and more aware that this magic quality in his playing was not so much the result of any deliberate and detailed pianistic planning on his part, as of a completely spontaneous, almost improvisatory approach to the keyboard. However, this spontaneity was combined with the most uncanny knowledge of the score, a knowledge that was almost pedantic in the accuracy of every detail of notation and, at the same time, immensely imaginative in the realization of the implications of every such detail. The keyboard and its mechanical mastery were taken for granted. Yet the most exhaustive and precise knowledge of the score was never accepted as complete. This knowledge was continually being renewed, even in the music he must have performed and heard performed by others for half a century.

"The performance itself was simply an act of translating what he heard so vividly, accurately and intensely with his mind's ear into a series of sounds audible to others. Naturally, if a finger slipped, the sound image would be marred, but it would never become distorted or destroyed. The enormous intensity and accuracy of his conception of the musical design always protected both the music and the performer. This supreme concentration on the "what" of music instead of the "how" of it was to me perhaps the most characteristic feature of his playing.

"As a teacher he would sometimes seem to distrust it. As if prompted by scruples of conscience he would suddenly suggest or even insist upon a regimen of technical exercises, thinking, I imagine: 'After all, I am supposed to teach this

100

boy how to handle the instrument; I really ought to do something about it.' However, his heart seldom seemed to be in it and his 'duty' done he would return to the music with renewed relish. Sometimes he would insist that the sound he imagined could be achieved only by some special pianistic device, by placing a finger upon the key in a certain specified manner. But often, in illustrating, he would do the exact opposite with his own fingers. It mattered little: the sound was invariably there when he played, no matter what was done to produce it.

"A typical lesson, as I remember it, would proceed somewhat as follows: First, all the inaccuracies of the student's reading would be corrected. If one misread an accent, a dynamic marking, a tempo change, Mr. Friedberg would correct it. This was a sort of preliminary procedure. The real lesson began when he examined the implied logical consequences of the printed instructions in the score. The student soon learned that for every printed marking in the score there were thousands of implied ones, the execution of which the composer takes for granted since he has a hard time imagining an unmusical performance. Otherwise, the composer would be forced to write a dissertation instead of a piece of music.

"Is this *crescendo* meant to be executed only for its printed duration or does it imply a carry-over into the next phrase? The harmonic and rhythmic patterns would be examined for a possible clue, other similar instances in the works of the same composer cited and played by Mr. Friedberg as examples, instances in chamber music, songs, orchestral works or operas, as well as other pianoforte works. What about a *ritard?* How much and how long? The same procedure would follow with more examples out of his seemingly inexhaustible memory.

"Yet all this search for accuracy never degenerated into pedantry, as it so easily could, because Carl Friedberg not only valued but cherished an instinctive musical reaction and would always rely on it as the final arbiter. Everything had to 'sound.' Everything had to be rhythmically pliable. Only when the music 'sounded' and moved to satisfy his innate, instinctive sense of fitness was the pedagogic argument of any consequence.

"The immense musical erudition, the equally immense pianistic experience, the thorough knowledge of the minutiae of the musical workshop were used only as a guide for the intuitive reaction, a guide that would at all times prevent the instinct from going contrary to the composer's written instructions and their logical, though unwritten, consequences.

"Thus his musical scholarship never seemed to interfere with his emotional re-experiencing of a piece of music. A piece heard, played, taught for perhaps fifty years seemed to keep for him the freshness of its emotional impact, often much more so than for a student who spent a few weeks studying it.

"His tastes in music were all-embracing. Any type and style of music would arouse his enthusiasm so long as it was well written, sincere and above mediocrity. His knowledge of the literature was encyclopaedic. Besides pianoforte music he seemed to know everything else equally well: operas, songs, oratorios, chamber music, symphonies, popular music, jazz, operettas, string and even wind soli. How he managed to know so much contemporary music always puzzled me, since, although I knew his enormous interest in all contemporary arts, I also knew that his eyesight was never too good. But he delighted in suggesting that I learn a piece that was just published by some composer of whom I had never heard, and would immediately sit down and play by memory some passages from it that had pleased him.

"His general culture seemed fully to match his musical knowledge. A phrase would often suggest to him a painting or a poem or a passage in a drama or a novel. He would always be able to identify them with utmost precision, even to the room in the museum where the painting could be seen, or the publisher of the volume in which the poem was contained.

"He was a sharp and witty critic with an excellent sense of humor and was extremely generous in his praise, whenever it was possible for him to praise anyone. He was equally generous with his time and would often spend many extra hours trying to help a student over some difficulties. The number of free lessons he gave must have been enormous, for he never asked for a fee from a student who interested him, if this student could ill afford to pay him.

"As a man he seemed to be interested in everything about him and encouraged his students to do likewise. As a pianist and a teacher of pianists he served as a living and unselfconscious example of the two truths which form the cornerstone of all musical performance.

"One is, that unless one learns to hear the piece of music mentally it is of little use to try to execute it with one's fingers. The other is that if one wishes to communicate the contents of the music one performs, the instinct must be allowed to guide the performer, but only after one's intellect absorbs and considers all there is to know about this piece of music."

VI

THE LATTER YEARS

(1946-1955)

1945 and 1946 were years of wild jubilation for many, for they brought an end to the most savage war in history. The termination of the strife, first in Europe and later in Asia, brought great changes in the lives of many. Among them was Carl Friedberg who now faced the second gravest moment of his artistic career. By reason of his age, 73, on extremely short notice, he was informed that his services at the Juilliard School were no longer needed.

Severance from his teaching positions left him, for the moment, stunned. In the best of health and at the peak of his mental powers, he was regarded by many as one of the greatest teachers in the world. To be counted as old, and therefore no longer useful, came to him as a severe shock.

When it became known that Friedberg had received notice that his services would be terminated at the end of the school term, a collective letter was sent to William Schuman * in May, 1946, bearing the signatures of many noted musicians, including Bruno Walter, Fritz Kreisler,

* Upon the resignation of Ernest Hutcheson, in 1945, as President of the Juilliard School, William Schuman, who had headed the Department of Music at Sarah Lawrence College, Bronxville, New York, was appointed to succeed him.

104

Walter Damrosch, Vladimir Horowitz, Myra Hess, Sir Adrian Boult, Adolph Busch, Daniel Gregory Mason and others, in which they expressed "regret and astonishment that Professor Carl Friedberg will not be with the Juilliard School for the coming year." The letter continued as follows:

We feel and we are sure wide circles will agree with us—that Professor Friedberg is one of the outstanding musicians of our time. He is not only a great performer, but also an eminent teacher and one of the most inspiring musical personalities of whom we have only a very few in the world today.

For many decades, Professor Friedberg has given proof of his unselfish devotion to the cause of music. Hundreds of fine musicians owe him their education. Many modern composers are indebted to him for having given first performances of their works. Audiences both here and in Europe have enjoyed Friedberg's authoritative interpretations of the great compositions of all times, and he has always been a stimulating factor in the musical life of this country.

We fail to understand that any musical institution that has the great fortune to call Professor Friedberg a member of its faculty would voluntarily dispense with his services. We are told that the Juilliard does not want to renew his contract because of his age. May we point out in this connection that there is no age limit in art. Especially in the field of music—creative and recreative—we know of many outstanding examples where great artists gave their best in their advanced years.

For all these reasons, we would consider the enforced retirement of Professor Friedberg an irreparable loss for music itself and above all for the younger generation which, now more than ever, needs a man of such world-wide experience and knowledge.

We urge you therefore, kindly to reconsider your decision and to make it possible for Professor Friedberg to continue his work on a level which will allow him to perform the same kind of distinguished services he has rendered for so many years.

We write to you personally because we are convinced that you will give full consideration to this matter which, in our opinion, is of the greatest importance for music as well as for the musical education in this country.

Regrettably this letter failed to convince the new administration of the Juilliard School that it should review its decision.

Displaying, as of old, his customary resilience, and recovering from this worst of all blows, Friedberg was heartened that all his pupils wished to remain in his class. He continued teaching at home during the winter and, for the next decade, was much sought after to conduct Master Classes in various parts of the United States: at the University of Kansas City (1946-1952); at the Juilliard Summer School (1946-1952), of which George A. Wedge was the first director; * the Detroit Institute of Musical Art; Winthrop College (Rock Hill, South Carolina); the Filmore Studios (Pittsburgh); University of Minnesota (Minneapolis); Augustana College (Sioux Falls, South Dakota); and at Bowling Green State University (Ohio). Juilliard's loss became the country's greater gain, for the artist-teacher now came in contact with pianists and teachers who form the backbone of piano-teaching in various sections of the United States.**

* After 1952, the Juilliard no longer maintained a summer school.
** To William Schuman's credit it must be said that as others of his excellent faculty reached their Seventies he found it difficult, if not impossible, to replace the high quality of their teaching and this convinced him that he should not enforce retirement regulations to the letter. Thus no longer is advancing age of an artist-teacher the sole basis for retirement from the Julliard School.

In all these cities Friedberg gave solo recitals, concerning which the Kansas City *Times* review of June, 1948 (when he was 75 years old), is typical:

> There was far more than mere musical pleasure in the ovation which a capacity crowd gave Carl Friedberg at the close of his all-Beethoven program last night at the Nelson Gallery of Art. There was veneration and esteem for one of the really great men of music,—a man who still plays a wonderful concert, because in his youth he learned how to play at the feet of the greatest pianists the world has known, and by the mastery he attained over the style of that golden age, brings the art of that period to the battered ears of a generation which seldom hears the piano played except as a percussive instrument.
>
> . . . seldom has an audience, heavily proportioned but by no means wholly composed of students and teachers, listened so intently and with such respect as was accorded Mr. Friedberg last night. (. . .) The ovation at the close continued loud and long, and though the program had been a long and difficult one, the master returned and played a short encore—a movement from the Beethoven sonata, Op. 31, No. 3.[1]

Friedberg arranged other worth-while events for his Master Classes, among which may be mentioned the appearance of two pianists from his New York Class, Marienka Michna and Jane Carlson, both of whom performed at the University of Kansas City in 1947. Miss Michna was heard in the complete piano (solo) works of Brahms (five recitals), and Miss Carlson gave a program of compositions by Hindemith, unusual recitals for that part of the country.

The change in attitude of what constituted "old age" in the Nineteenth as compared with the Twentieth Century is noted in the incident of Liszt as related by the London

Musical Times in 1883. Liszt, having been requested to take part in a concert given at Paris on behalf of the inundated districts of Alsace-Lorraine, wrote a letter to the Committee expressing his inability to assist on the occasion in question, and added:

> As a man of 72 I am, unfortunately, an invalid as regards pianoforte playing. I could not—at least in public —risk the reputation of my ten fingers, unpractised as they have now been for years, without meeting with a certain fiasco. I have no doubt whatever on this point, and, having regard to my great age, am determined to abstain from playing in public altogether for the future.[2]

Although Friedberg did not perform at either Town Hall or Carnegie Hall after 1945, he was heard in New York several times thereafter at the Juilliard Summer School concerts of which the Chopin recital, given in August, 1949, and that of July, 1951, in which he played works by Mozart, Beethoven, Mendelssohn, Brahms and Chopin left outstanding memories. The latter concert, according to Marion Bauer, ". . . was given before an audience which was unmindful of the terrific heat while listening to this amazing artist interpret music as only he can." [3]

At Bowling Green University (Ohio) where he conducted a Master Class in 1953, at the age of 81, following his recital there which comprised the same works as his 1951 recital at Juilliard, Wolfgang Stresemann wrote:

> A piano recital by Carl Friedberg is now, as always, one of the most magnificent of musical experiences. (. . .) He is a miracle of vitality, musicality and genuine pianistic genius. It sounds incredible: nobody surpasses him in inwardness and power of expression; his fire and

Plate 8
Carl Friedberg in his studio at Baden Baden, 1926

Plate 9

Trio at Baden Baden, 1930. Gregor Piatigorsky, Carl Flesch and Carl Friedberg

temperament are a challenge to all comers, and technically he fulfills every wish. (. . .)

(. . .) Without exaggeration one may say that from him almost all the other pianists, whether young or experienced, could learn. One who has made masterly music for more than six decades as he has done, can indeed point the right way. (. . .)

It speaks well for America that especially the younger generation of musicians is enthusiastic about this unique artist. The number of Friedberg pupils is endless, and none of them will ever forget the great knowledge and accomplishments of their teacher, his incomparable pedagogic talent, and especially his never-waning enthusiasm. (. . .) His enthusiastic devotion to music is contagious. Those who are around him not only learn a craft, but they experience with him the true greatness of music, its unique spiritual significance, its eternal message for mankind. No wonder that Friedberg's educational activity has such a lasting effect.[4]

In his last years Friedberg loved two things especially: to have his pupils around him as much as possible, and his improvising. "I spent my 77th birthday reading Richard Strauss's scores," he wrote Lonny Epstein, on September 19, 1949. "The masterly instrumentation, the clarity of the polyphony and the phrase elaboration (Satzkunst) are an ever renewed source of admiration. There are works which have not found sufficient attention as (f.i.), *Macbeth* (which I conducted in Wiesbaden) and the two splendid songs with orchestra for baritone: 'Nocturne' (Dehmel) and 'Nachtlicher Gang' (Rückert)."

The high regard and genuine endearment that Friedberg, in turn, generated in the hearts of his pupils is noted in a letter that William Masselos, one of America's outstanding younger pianists, wrote to the man to whom he came as a pupil at the age of 12, and with whom he studied for eleven or twelve years. Masselos's letter, dated August 15, 1953, thanks his former teacher for remembering his recent birthday and ends with an expression of esteem:

Dear Oom Carl: *

The volume of Scriabine Sonatas is the most welcome present you could have given me. Now I finally have them all, and I shall certainly remember your program suggestion of three sonatas plus the Reger Variations—a most unique program. I wish I could have the chance to record some of the sonatas. . . . How I'd love to do the Satie too!

As I get older (and older) I place increasing value on the capacity of a man to be gentle, kind, and thoughtful —which is always a good yard-stick to judge his true inner nature by—perhaps even more so than his intelligence. The greatest things in the world! Thank you for setting an example for all of us, Oom Carl. A beautiful example.

With loving thanks
from

Bill

Friedberg held the lifelong belief that an artist who is also a teacher should uphold and transmit the knowledge and ideals of the past to succeeding generations, so that the great line of artistic continuity will be maintained. He clearly stated his views on this obligation and scathingly condemned the inferior quality of art produced in recent years in an excerpt taken from a letter dated October 14, 1947, and addressed to Lonny Epstein.

The more the spiritlessness of the 'Century of the Common Man' with its vulgar shouting and its barbaric

* "Oom" is the Dutch familiar expression for "Uncle."

lack of culture is a menace to the beauty and glory of music, the more it is the obligation of the champions of the 'Wahren, Schönen, Guten' (the True, the Beautiful, the Good) to preserve and to cherish all the noble things which have come down to us. That does not mean we should shut our eyes to what is good in new things—on the contrary—Progress is vertical and we have to build new layers on top of the old ones.

As a concrete example of this principle, Friedberg sought in his teaching to rekindle the art of improvisation.* He often demonstrated his own superior gifts in this direction to his pupils, particularly to the ones who had the instinct to compose. He frequently asserted the belief that a performer who also composed possessed a more sensitive ability to interpret music than one who did not; for the former, necessarily working more intimately with the materials of music, is able to understand their various implications and subtle shades of meaning more easily than the latter. He often stated that one of the greatest assets of "popular dance music" is in its reliance on improvisation which, at best, lifts an often ordinary melody to new and heretofore unrealized heights.

Busoni, he recalled on one occasion, said that he had written so many transcriptions that even his original works sounded to him like transcriptions, for, "after all," he quoted the Italian pianist as saying, "even the first jotting down of a composition is already a transcription of the composer's first thought!"

Taking, for example, a basic primitive rhythm, a catchy motive of some composer, or simply the inflection of a particular spoken word or phrase, Friedberg had the gift (and skill) to improvise works in whatever style he chose at the

* To improvise, according to Webster, is "to compose, recite, sing or play without previous study or preparation; to contrive or devise on the spur of the moment."

moment—French, German, Russian, or American idiom—in classic, romantic, or modern vein, often stimulating his pupils to attempt the same.

As in his youth, he played Rubinstein's "Valse Caprice" note-perfect, without ever having seen the score and only after one hearing, so also in later years he reproduced the Prokofieff sonatas and Martinu piano pieces which he himself never performed publicly but did so for his pupils, merely from hearing them performed. When one of his students (Maro Ajemian) played Prokofieff's third piano concerto for the Russian master on his American tour in 1933, Prokofieff congratulated Friedberg on the orchestral version of the score which he played "from memory" at the accompanying second piano. The composer was greatly impressed when he learned that Friedberg's "study" of the orchestral score had been his two hearings of the work which Prokofieff himself had played as soloist with the Philharmonic-Symphony only a few days before.

To his pupils Friedberg suggested that they improvise cadenzas to concerti, as Mozart always did, reminding them that not until Beethoven's time was it regarded necessary to write out all the notes to be played. He also declared that even if one devoted only thirty minutes daily to extemporizing, utilizing one's best concentration and musical instincts, amazing results could be attained.

Except for its preservation as the basis of "progressive jazz," he noted, and also of folk music, the art of improvisation, or extemporizing, with a few exceptions, has virtually disappeared. What has caused this art, so nobly served by the pre-Bach organists, J. S. Bach, Handel, Mozart, Beethoven, Mendelssohn and Liszt to fall into disuse?

Friedberg held that there were two reasons for this: In the first place, during the Eighteenth Century, music functioned in the aristocratic atmosphere of the church and court. When Bach improvised for Frederick the Great, he improvised for a King who was himself a discerning musician

112

and who knew enough to have given Bach the theme that became the basis for "The Art of the Fugue." Where in today's democratic age is to be found the leader of any country who knows a great deal about the art of music and who is as proficient on the instrument of his choice as was Frederick on the flute?

Secondly, he noted, Liszt was the last of the great giants of improvisation and it was during his lifetime that public concerts, as we know them, first came into being. It would then appear that with the introduction of the set, or fixed program and the vogue established by the French in playing entire recitals from memory, without notes, that the art of improvisation began to decline, simply for the lack of time to prepare such exacting programs and yet devote the daily hours necessary to keep up one's facility in extemporizing.

After hearing the American pianist, Grace Castagnetta play in New York, in 1949, Friedberg was so enraptured with her ability to extemporize that he invited her, almost immediately, to play for his class, for he found her the perfect example, in contemporary times, of a true improviser. She came at the appointed time and, afterwards, in a letter dated December 18, 1949, wrote him of her pleasure at having performed for him again.

Dear, dear Carl Friedberg,

How shall I ever be able to tell you what a rich and rewarding experience Friday evening was? I, too, am inarticulate when I should be eloquent—and failed to say all the things I felt. It was a great honor to be asked by you to play for your Master Class—to understand how deeply honored you would have been to know that I grew up—in Cologne in an atmosphere that worshipped and admired your great art. Your name at the Hochschule stood for everything that every young pianist strived and aspired toward. When it was announced that you were coming back to Germany and would play in Düsseldorf

113

(Beethoven C minor Concerto) I saved for weeks to get to that concert. Your playing made an indelible impression—which I'll treasure always. All this I thought of and would have liked to have related to your young disciples. Forgive me for not having done so.

Always you have given me renewed faith and hope and belief, ideals to live up to, fresh courage to hold high the torch. For this there can be no mere 'Thank you' but a genuine desire to go forth and do likewise.

For Christmas I wish for you the realization that all you have poured into the world makes it possible for more people to say and mean 'peace on earth.' All my love and gratitude,

Grace

It is doubtful that Carl Friedberg thereafter ever missed one of Miss Castagnetta's New York recitals and following the one she played in November, 1953, he wrote her the following note in which he has paraphrased a quotation from the German poet, Kopisch:

After the concert
Nov. 28th, '53

Dear Friend,

There is something so wondrous and marvelous in your playing—nobody but you has it—which is best expressed in the words of a German Ballad by Loewe— 'Der Noeck'—the water ghost who appears emerging from the river every night when children are at play on the shore and sings accompanying himself on the lyre and of whom the poet says:

'Er konnte die Kinder lachen und weinen machen, mit seinem Singen.' *

* Translation: "He could make the children laugh and weep with his singing."

God bless you, you angel
Carl Friedberg

Two tributes accorded the artist for his unique contribution to the musical life of America, both of which brought him much joy, occurred in 1950: one, in the form of a personal expression by several hundreds of his former pupils, both here and abroad; the other, a civic honor conferred upon him by one of our large Mid-Western cities.

The first was the formation by his former pupils as an expression of their love and devotion to him, of the Carl Friedberg Alumni Association—later known as the Carl Friedberg Music Foundation—whose purpose was the establishment of scholarship grants in order to provide gifted young pianists of limited financial means with an opportunity to study with their Master. With Claudio Arrau, Gaby Casadesus, Robert Casadesus, Dame Myra Hess, Otto Klemperer, Dimitri Mitropoulos and Rudolf Serkin as Patrons, the Foundation annually gave a series of spring concerts in New York from 1950-1956, the proceeds of which were contributed to the Foundation's scholarship fund. Of the approximately ten young pianists who were aided in this manner by the Foundation, Bruce Hungerford, John Thomas Covelli, and Silvi Lindström are successfully pursuing concert careers. With the passing of the great pianist in 1955, the Foundation raised funds to purchase his valuable library from Mrs. Friedberg which, in 1957, they presented as The Carl Friedberg Memorial Library to Columbia University. Successfully terminating the purpose of its existence, the Foundation is no longer active.

Friedberg's final orchestral appearances were made with the Youngstown (Ohio) and Toledo Symphony Orchestras. With the former group, John Kreuger, conductor, he played in 1954, at the age of 82, the Schumann Concerto. With the Toledo Orchestra, Wolfgang Stresemann, conductor, he performed no less than three times: in 1950, he was soloist in the Schumann Concerto; in 1951, the Brahms B flat; and in 1954, the Beethoven "Emperor" Concerto.

As a token of the city's veneration and affection for the great artist at the conclusion of his performance of the Schumann Concerto (January 18, 1950), the Mayor of Toledo, the Honorable Michael V. DiSalle, presented Friedberg with a key to the city accompanied by a scroll, which made him an honorable and honored citizen of Toledo.

Terming the presentation ". . . a fitting crowning of an evening of music that was unusual in many ways," Frederick J. Kountz, critic of the *Times,* had the following to say regarding the performance of the Schumann Concerto:

> I have thought frequently that one who plays this music fully, who makes it sing out, must not only be a musician of stature, but must be as well a person of consequence, a warm person imbued with a bountiful love of mankind; a person of no pretense; a person of integrity, of taste, and of deep feeling for the wonderful beauty which Schumann created. One might even say that the performer must be as much as possible like Carl Friedberg.
>
> Mr. Friedberg has become almost a regular visitor to our city. And the extent of the honor and privilege of our association with him grows on every occasion upon which he presents himself again to us. We learn that he and his music are of this generation, of generation past, of generations to come. They are ageless and changeless and beautiful in a manner that is deeply moving. Of Mr. Friedberg's playing last night there is nothing more we should say, nothing more that should be said than this: he is a great musician and a very great man.[5]

The second morning following, on the Editorial Page of the *Blade,* appeared a lengthy tribute from which several excerpts are taken, addressed to

116

Our Honorary Citizen

There was something at once touching and inspiring about the simple ceremony on the stage of the Peristyle of Toledo's Museum of Art Wednesday evening when Carl Friedberg, (. . .) was made an honorary citizen of this city in whose musical life he has played such an important and helpful part.

It was a small token of the affection in which this fine musician is held by Toledoans. Yet how better could a great city express its appreciation of what Mr. Friedberg has done—as an artist, as an adviser, as one willing to help in any way possible—to advance its civic music program? . . .

Equally apparent is the honor which is Toledo's in Mr. Friedberg's acceptance of the status of honorary citizen. For this man, this vital, energetic, bubbling over man, is a figure unique in the world of music. . . .

This, then is Toledo's honorary citizen—a great man, a great musician, who unites the promise of the present with the glories of the past in music. If our city honors him, he honors it still more.[6]

It is doubtful that the pianist ever regarded himself as old for the reason that his mind was at all times exceptionally alert and clear and his health generally robust, except for the illness of 1924. This is characteristically illustrated in a conversation he had with Wolfgang Stresemann in 1950 (when the pianist was 78) in the presence of Aline Jean Treanor, then music critic of the Toledo *Blade*. At that time the Toledo Orchestra, like almost all others, was having financial difficulties and Friedberg said to its conductor: "As soloist with your orchestra next season I would like to give my services—but instead, can only cut my price some, as I have my future to think of."

Although most great pianists recorded extensively so that their discography today lends a certain artistic immortality to them, Friedberg did not wish to leave the memory of his playing by this means. In the first place he was never satisfied with the sound of the piano even at best as it was reproduced on recordings. A far more important reason is that he did not wish to have his conception of a given work forever stamped by one set, or fixed interpretation achieved in a recording session. For him art existed as the sublime improvisation of an intensive mood which must always remain variable and flexible. Because of this attitude he was dissatisfied with the result of the Liszt and Chopin pieces he "recreated" for Duo Art piano rolls early in his career. His sole recording,* made at 81, contains pieces by Brahms, an original improvisation of his own and, according to Herbert Kupfferberg, "a performance of Schumann's 'Kinderscenen' that for sheer poetic beauty outmatches any other current recording of this work, save possibly the Gieseking. This is piano playing that ascends the heights of artistry." [7]

Referring to the short improvisation contained on one side of the record, Friedberg afterwards commented to a pupil: "When I sat down to play this little piece, I had no idea what I was going to play. When I had finished, I had no recollection of what I had played, but when I heard it played back, it sounded good to me, all of one piece."

Evidence of Friedberg's still potent mental powers that kept him fully abreast of his time, is revealed by his last article written in 1954 for *Musical America*. A sympathetic approach to the problems that confront young pianists today with some helpful suggestions for their solution, his article is appropriately titled:

The Technical Aspects of Playing
Must Be Subconscious
By Carl Friedberg
(As told to Rafael Kammerer)

"Like everything else in life today, the learning processes have been speeded up. The gifted young pianist of the

* Zodiac Record, LP Z-1001.

present is mentally more alert and learns faster, perhaps, than his counterpart of thirty or forty years ago; but he is also forced to develop under social and economic pressures undreamed of in former years. He is squeezed and buffeted from all sides. Besides maintaining a fast pace, he must face keener and stiffer competition, and, with the cost of living so high, he has a hard time making ends meet even when he is successful in getting engagements.

"Many brilliant young pianists, in order to make a living, are compelled by necessity to spend precious time—musical or otherwise—on tasks that are merely money-making ones not at all conducive to artistic growth. The development of a truly great pianist is an unhurried process. It not only takes time; it requires a certain peace of mind. No one can concentrate on the inner meanings of great works of art with a mind harassed by a thousand fleeting, crowding impressions. And that is where the student of yesterday had the advantage over those of today. He had his problems, to be sure, but he had fewer distractions.

"I am not a pessimist, nor do I care to dwell in the past. We live in the world of today and must make the best of it. If sometimes I fear for the future of the piano, that is because I love it so. People are *stuffed* with music. You cannot go anywhere now without having it blared into your ears, usually mixed with all sorts of extraneous noises. The enormous inflation of quantity will kill the quality of our art. Overcoming the apathy produced by excess is another challenge the young performer must meet.

"The aspiring pianist should also have more than one iron in the fire. When pupils come to me, the first question I ask is: 'Do you aim for public performance?' When they say 'yes,' I ask them what else they are capable of doing. If a pupil shows ability in public speaking, for instance, I encourage him to be a lecturer on music as well as a performer of it. Another may be able to write intelligently, and so on. I do this because I believe it is the teacher's duty not only to guide and help his pupils develop as artist-performers, but also to leave no stone unturned that may aid them in getting a foothold on the ladder of success. It takes will power and a fanatical zeal to succeed today—and faith in oneself.

"When an opportunity presents itself, I never allow a pupil of mine to ignore it. Every opportunity to perform in public, or private must be seized. Of course, I am speaking of the advanced pupil who is already in the artist class and is capable of giving a recital or of performing a concerto with orchestra. Orchestral conductors often call on me to supply a solo pianist, usually on short notice, to perform one of the standard concertos in the repertory—it may be to pinch hit for a big name artist who is indisposed, or to play the solo part in a new work that particular conductor wishes to present.

"Whichever it is, when I am asked whether I have any one in mind I always answer 'Certainly!' even when I have not the slightest idea at the moment who it might be. If it is a new work, one with which I am not familiar, I get a copy of the score, select the pupil most likely to learn it in the given time—usually two or three days—and we go to work on it, spending as many hours as necessary. Many new works for piano and orchestra have been given their first performances by pupils of mine. Tilly Indianer, then seventeen years old, introduced the Prokofieff Third Concerto here in 1927. Another pupil of mine, Marshall Wrubel, now professor of astrophysics at Indiana University, gave the first performance of the Stravinsky Concerto, as did Maro Ajemian the Khachaturian.

CHAMPION OF NEW MUSIC

"I have always been a champion of contemporary music. When I was at the Juilliard School I gave what I called 'One-Man Shows'—recitals, in which my pupils played, devoted to the music of a single composer. Ravel, Eugene

Goossens, Leopold Godowsky, Beryl Rubinstein, and Rach-maninoff, were some of the composers represented. More-over, there were many fine works played that one seldom, or never, hears; such as the Cyril Scott *Sonata,* a fine, vigorous, work full of surprising rhythmic changes.

"I expect the pupils who come to me for lessons to be well prepared, to love music, and to be willing to work. Where the foundation is lacking, I use Clementi's *Gradus ad Parnassum* and Czerny's *Art of Finger Dexterity,* along with Isidor Philipp. I also use the modern etudes of Ernst Toch and Béla Bartók, the Roy Harris 'Toccata' and a wonderful 'Passacaglia' by Vittorio Giannini, all of which are fine music as well as excellent studies. Add to this list the 'Canonic Studies' by the young American composer-pianist of the NBC Symphony, John La Montaine. I still consider the music of Carl Maria von Weber excellent for developing the brilliant romantic style of playing. As for scale practice, while I believe in it, I do not insist upon it unless the hands are stiff. Finger dexterity, after all, is more a matter of the mind than of the fingers.

"Composers sometimes make their piano music more difficult than it need be. Clara Schumann, when I was studying with her, made the interesting observation that Robert Schumann made his piano music too difficult only after he had injured his fingers. I consider the first and third movements of his *Sonata in G Minor* to be among the most difficult things in all piano music.

"Pupils in general are too impatient; they do not want to persevere with a piece until they have mastered it com-pletely. Teachers, especially in smaller communities away from large centers, are apt to stick too much to conventional teaching material. In my lectures before teacher-groups in various parts of the country, and in my classes for teachers, I try to show them how they can make their work more inter-esting to their pupils, as well as to themselves, by composing their own teaching pieces tailored to fit the needs of the individual young student. I show them how to improvise short pieces and then tell them to teach their pupils to do the same, or, if they prefer, write them out for the pupil.

"One of the questions I am asked to answer most frequently in my lecture-recitals is: "How can I overcome stage fright?" I *cure* a case of stage fright in five minutes. Like a doctor, I first find out the cause. Is it vanity, or is it a bad conscience? There are no others! It is the former when the performer thinks more of himself than he does of the music. Concentration on the work in hand kills vanity. It is a bad conscience when the performer is not fully prepared. So I say, be prepared, trust in the Lord, and do not let your conscious mind interfere with the automatic reflex actions. The technical aspects of playing must be subconscious.

"In closing, I should like to air a few of my pet ideas. I would like to see a diffusion of opportunity for young musicians throughout the smaller communities of this country instead of the concentration we now have in the big cities. This will have to come in one way or another. Solfeggio should be taught to every child in the public schools, in the early grades, as an ear-training development for good listening. We have plenty of good performers but not nearly enough good listeners willing and able to enjoy what they hear. Finally, everyone who owns a radio or television set should contribute one dollar a year to a general fund set up to help musicians and to aid the cause of music in general." [8]

Although for many years he had no wish to return to his native country because of the terrible crimes Hitler and his henchmen had perpetrated on the German people, and also because he did not wish to view the war destruction, nevertheless, about 1952 Friedberg began to toy with the idea of once more returning to Europe.

Two years later, in 1954 he went to Switzerland, visiting

Lucerne and Lugano, then on to Baden Baden where he spent two delightful weeks. He found the latter place one of the few in Germany that seemed not to have changed. Once again he stood underneath the branches of the 200-year-old trees growing along the banks of the River Oos and strolled through the Kurgarten, admiring the colorful flowers. In the center of war-torn Germany, Baden Baden was a veritable paradise. He went again to Rumpelmayer's where he enjoyed as of old his favorite little cakes and patisseries. All the shop-keepers remembered him and welcomed home again the Herr Professor.

Many of his former German students, some of whom had studied with him fifty years before, came to see him and to ask advice; and for all he suggested musical works which they should now study!

He was invited to play on the radio at both Baden Baden and Cologne so that a larger German audience might hear him again but postponed all opportunities to play until the following summer, when he would be "in better form." Friedberg was refreshed by this visit with old friends and former pupils and left Baden Baden feeling newly made.

After a busy winter in New York the Friedbergs left in August, 1955, on the Conte Savoia, for Genoa, from which port they were to proceed to Munich, where many American and German students awaited him. Following this he was to go to Baden Baden for a broadcast throughout Europe of the Schumann Concerto with the Südwestdeutsche Rundfunk Orchestra. Before his departure two New York appearances in the fall and winter had been announced: he was to appear as soloist in the Twenty-Fifth Anniversary Season of the National Orchestral Association, Leon Barzin, conductor, at which on November 8, in the first concert of the season, he was to play the Schumann Concerto in commemoration of the Association's first concert twenty-five years ago when he had performed that work; and he was to appear as assisting-artist with the Budapest Quartet in a program of his choosing at the Kaufmann Auditorium (Y.M.H.A.) on January 14, 1956.

Aboard ship, which took one week in crossing, and on which he had expected to enjoy a good rest and brief vacation before resuming his strenuous summer activities, he contracted bronchitis from exposure to too much draft and from not having dressed warmly enough when he strolled, or sun-bathed on deck. On landing at Genoa he was worse, and his wife took him to a sanatorium in Merano where he was nursed under the care of a capable doctor.

Here he lingered comfortably until September 9th, conscious and fully alert to the end, when his once strong and ever courageous heart finally ceased, only nine days short of his eighty-third birthday. His death came as a shock and great loss to his many pupils and friends, all of whom regarded him as indestructible, for he had outlived almost all the pianists of his own generation and beyond.

All over the world the press took note of his passing. One of New York City's radio stations, WQXR, broadcast remarks by Wolfgang Stresemann on the life and career of the great artist, stressing his irreplaceable loss not only to music but especially to the younger generation of pianists. The program ended with the playing of the master's recording of works by Schumann and Brahms.

Serkin replaced Friedberg as assisting artist with the Budapest Quartet and their eloquent performances of the Schumann and Brahms piano quintets were fitting memorials to the great teacher-pianist by his beloved colleagues. Although his final resting place is the little cemetery of Merano, under the sunny skies of Italy, the memory of Carl Friedberg, who was both teacher and friend to his pupils, remains for them and for all others who knew him intimately a shining beacon which cannot be extinguished and whose warm glow does not diminish.

Plate 10

Gerda and Carl Friedberg at Ascona, 1933

Plate 11

Faculty of the Juilliard Graduate School, New York City, 1936 (Courtesy of the Juilliard School) Seated—left to right—Frederick Jacobi,* Bernard Wagenaar, Edouard Dethier,* Edith Braun, Madeleine Marshall, Oscar Wagner (Dean), Rosina Lhévinne, Ernest Hutcheson * (President), Anna E. Schön-René,* Olga Samaroff Stokowski,* Florence Page Kimball, Charles Hackett,* Willem Willeke.* Standing—left to right—Albert Spalding,* Vittorio Giannini, Robert Simon, Francis Rogers,* James Friskin, Louis Persinger, Hans Letz, Carl Friedberg,* Felix Salmond,* Josef Lhévinne,* Alexander Siloti,* Paul Reimers,* Georges Barrère,* Frederick Kiesler, Leopold Sachse.

* deceased

VII

GLIMPSES INTO THE TEACHING OF
CARL FRIEDBERG
AS RELATED BY HIS PUPILS

(1903-1955)

There are many reasons why Carl Friedberg was destined to be ranked among the great teachers. Paramount is the fact that he understood the true basis of the art of teaching: to foster in the mind of the student a deep love for his subject and an unquenchable desire to learn.

To him music was the means of transforming the drabness of every-day living into something beautiful, interesting and exciting. He was of the firm opinion that the pursuit of the art of music developed character, lifting its devotees to higher emotional and intellectual levels and that, through loving and propagating the art, one learned to demand order and beauty as essentials of daily living.

He taught through inspiration, though demanding strict adherence to the score. His aim was to set the student to discover for himself the meaning of the notes on the printed page and to delve more deeply into the thought of the composer. He had extraordinary ability to portray in language the student might best comprehend what precisely would enable him to play with freedom and authority. He encouraged his students to read the great literature of all time and to study examples of the best painting, sculpture and architecture. Except in certain contemporary works, he did not wish anything to sound harsh, and he often advised his students that even *fortissimo* passages must sound noble, never belligerent.

In his latter years Carl Friedberg was concerned with the artist of today. He never wished to compare artists, believing that what each personality projected was a quality of expression totally unlike that of any other performer. Although he did not tolerate inadequate technique, nevertheless, he used technique as a means to an end and deplored the current worship of speed for its own sake, typical of the playing of so many of the younger pianists. In the concert-hall he observed that many present-day artists do not trouble to study and re-study the music they play and often reveal that they have not had access to the original scores of the masters.* For these and other reasons he thought that many interpretations are seldom profound and that the pianists of today and tomorrow are in danger of becoming dillettantes.

Lonny Epstein has said that the greatness and effectiveness of Carl Friedberg's teaching consisted in his having no method at all, except the principle of applying hundreds of different methods adapted to the individual personalities and needs of as many students.

There were, of course, certain basic technical requirements, with the accent on accuracy, clarity, and above all tone quality,—as was reflected in his own playing. Vagueness of any kind he refused to tolerate any more than a pedantic approach, which he abhorred. With regard to the Chopin "Etude" *Op*. 25, *No*. 12, he said to a student: "I insist upon hearing every note."

He kindled the imagination of the student by evoking,

* For the piano works of Mozart and Beethoven Friedberg insisted that his students have access to the Urtext edition; for Schumann's works, the Clara Schumann edition; for Brahms' works, the Simrock edition.

on the spur of the moment, associations of mood and character with certain poems, picturizing, for instance, the second theme of the "Rondo" of Beethoven's G Major Concerto as ". . . a vine clinging around a tree"; or comparing the tempestuous "Scherzo" of *Op.* 110 to "a stormy late fall day with the leaves whirling around."

But what made Friedberg a truly *great* teacher was an inexplainable capacity, which might well be called a "magnetic power" to unearth and develop the innermost and hidden traces of talent in his students, giving them a degree of self-confidence which more often than not resulted in unexpected accomplishments, carrying them beyond their capacities, so to speak.

In addition, his warm personality and penetrating human understanding caused his students to come to him with their troubles and problems and find a sympathetic ear and helpful advice. The imprint of his influence penetrated far beyond the sphere of the purely musical and was decisive in forming their personalities.

Were his students interested in all facets of learning? Were they tolerant and kindly people? Were they sincere toward others and toward their own responsibilities? They learned that generosity of person was as important in the re-creation of music as agility in playing fast passages. They learned how grandeur of spirit emanates during performance.

The stamina and self-discipline of this man in the face of age and waning bodily strength was a spiritual enlightenment for his students. Was his hand wracked with arthritic pain? He would find yet another way to play the Brahms B flat Concerto unfettered. No storms or heat waves would keep this venerable gentleman from the head of his piano class. Never was time a factor, and he spared himself nothing when it came to extra help and coaching for the deserving. No aspect of his students' welfare found him disinterested. Were their gloves warm enough? Had they a convenient practice room and balanced meals?

To one student who was seriously ill with influenza he sent a hamper of nourishing delicacies, so that on the first few days upon returning home from the hospital the student might concentrate all his energy on gaining strength for a quick recovery. For one of his most gifted young pianists who was in financial straits, Friedberg not only paid the expenses connected with his New York debut recital but invited an audience to hear the young man in whom he greatly believed. He made it possible for other young artists to be engaged for European tours and was constantly engrossed with plans to help all his students attain their highest artistic fulfillment.

"Noblesse oblige," they were often reminded—the obligation to be humble and subservient to one's talent and art. Who can forget the stimulation of class sessions? All were bound to learn what the others studied; all could be expected to be criticized starkly, if constructively, before any students present. There could be no pretense or false pride. Students were asked candidly to appraise colleagues, and critics, in turn, were appraised by the teacher, the fairness and merit of their suggestions always lucidly dissected. Integrity of musical thought and achievement always superseded personal considerations.

Frequently after class lessons, Friedberg invited his students to luncheon at the historic Claremont Inn, in those days situated opposite the Juilliard School. Afterwards, if the weather permitted, all took a short stroll on Riverside Drive before resuming the afternoon's schedule. Never losing an opportunity to elucidate a musical principle from another point of view he, on one occasion, pointed to the recently completed George Washington bridge and said: "Young ladies and gentlemen! If you would learn true, controlled, uninterrupted legato, regard carefully that beautiful bridge," a remark none ever forgot.

"If one is in doubt about the way a phrase should sound,

one should imagine it being sung by a first-class singer," Carl Friedberg often said. "Immediately the notes will fall into the proper perspective of the phrase."

This also conveyed to him a clear indication of the correct tempo in slow-playing works. "It must not be played more slowly," he said, "than you are able to sing the phrase in one breath. Beyond that point the flow of the music is in great danger of being arrested—even with the best legato touch—and an unnatural, dull quality settles on the music."

Friedberg's conception of legato playing, the sliding in and out on the surface of the keys (with a downward rotation of the knuckles) from one note to another, resulted, when properly executed, in the smoothest transfer of weight from one finger to another. To him true legato was inseparable from first-class pianism.

Though he asked for physical action on the part of the student, in the transfer of weight from one finger to another, this was possible to attain only through the awakening of the student's inner consciousness and demanded the greatest mental and physical concentration along with extreme sensitivity. Thus the inner ear gradually learned to hear the sound for which the young player was continually searching.

Although many pianists think that once a tone is struck, nothing can change its quality, Carl Friedberg held that under certain conditions one could achieve various effects by means of "tone manipulation." He illustrated this by playing a note of long duration, giving a slight rebound to the key after having struck it which resulted in a "floating" quality of sound. To one pupil he explained the process by which he obtained this particular effect: After the key is struck it should not be grounded to its base but released a few degrees, at the same time releasing the arm-weight or pressure, but without removing the finger all the way from the key, so that the vibrations of the strings may

129

"open up" and permit the sound to travel up and outward. He applied this concept in his playing of Chopin's E flat "Nocturne," utilizing this technique, of course, only on the longer sustained notes of the melody. Those who heard him play the slow movement of the Brahms B flat Concerto will recall the ravishing, sensuous, floating legato-tone which he projected by the means described above. That this principle also works without the use of the pedal may be comprehended by applying it to the playing of the opening phrases of Aaron Copland's first of the *Four Piano Blues.*

Another adaptation of this idea is found in Friedberg's manner of making a dynamic change (fp) on a single note, octave, or chord. After the key is struck forcefully it should not be grounded to its base, but released with the aid of the damper pedal pressed down and lifted, perhaps several times in succession, depending on the length of the note played, while the fingers still cling to the keys, so that the vibrations of the strings are gradually released. This principle can be applied in various ways to achieve certain effects, i.e., the opening measures of the last movement of Schubert's *Sonata in B Flat Major* (the left-hand octave "G" with dynamic markings of *fp*), where, letting the key bounce and catching it again toneless before changing the pedal, produces the effect of a controlled diminishing of the sound.

In regard to playing with a "high upper arm," which has been sometimes misunderstood, Friedberg used this position for the playing of light and delicate passages, without arm weight. Endurance, he suggested, may be gained from the study and practice of the Liszt *Etudes,* especially the F minor and "Mazeppa" *Etudes,* which employ the use of the entire arm.

The Master held the belief that regardless of the amount of talent, any pianist could and *should* become a good craftsman. Perhaps this idea stemmed from his Germanic background which emphasized good craftsmanship in any line of work: one should take pride and have sincerity in doing honest work. "Beauty comes after exactness," he often remarked.

Even in the shorter summer sessions Friedberg always demanded a high standard of concentrated work. To an advanced player he assigned three large works to be learned in the five-week interval prior to a six-weeks summer session. These were the Schubert "Wanderer Phantasie," the Schumann Concerto and the Beethoven G Major Concerto. For the last named work the student was to improvise his own cadenzas. When the young man's face registered surprise at the large assignment, Friedberg shook an admonishing finger: "Yes," he said, "if you study with me, you have to work!"

With the beginning of the summer session the Master therefore already knew that particular student's capacity for work, his rate of learning, his ability for self-direction and self-reliance, so that the young man made enormous progress with his summer's study, polishing and refining his performances of these prepared works to a high, artistic level.

Many pianists who worked with Carl Friedberg, especially in summer sessions, were teachers who had stopped playing in public. He thought that the time-worn excuse of "no time to practice" was taking the line of least resistance and encouraged teachers to play in public, "to put on your best musical clothes before your students." He stressed the importance of retaining "the attitude of public performance," so that they might be of greater help to their students.

In a letter to one of his pupils, written during the last years of his life, Friedberg defined the responsibilities of a teacher and also indicated the advantages to be gained by the young student in presenting a first New York recital:

Oct. 31, 1952

Dear Malcolm (Frager):

Being an educator in art and all that belongs to it is a kind of trusteeship, the instructor being under an

131

obligation to do a complete job with the student en trusted to him, and the student and those who are responsible for his education working to co-operate with the teacher, whenever necessary.

A Town Hall recital for a debutant means, as the situation prevailing in New York is at present, to be criticized by press and public. It does not necessarily mean yet, even if the reception by both press and public has been most favorable, that an artist is 'finished.' Who ever is? It is rather a test and a mile-stone on the road to the future. If a Town Hall recital is postponed for another year, the young artist should fill the time by working hard and doing his best to grow and make still further progress. A recital program, kneaded and manipulated a full year ahead of a New York recital is the best preparation for a good result.

While Friedberg's teaching was never dogmatic but remained free and improvisational like his playing, he did insist on the following nuances:

(1) Play longer notes a shade louder than shorter ones;
(2) With regard to phrases that start with an upbeat, or anacrusis, the phrase must begin softer than the first important down-beat in order to lead the music to expressive and culminating focal points;
(3) The note following an accent should be diminished in sound;
(4) Concerning the playing of a melodic note in the right hand which is heard over a heavily accented bass note, a principle he attributed to Tausig, he suggested that one play the right hand (which utilizes the shorter strings of the piano) an instant before the left, which would then be heard in the proper perspective without banging. This suggestion may be applied to Beethoven's

Sonata in B Flat Major, Op. 22, the "Adagio" movement, (Measures 34-38) where the *sforzando (sf)* is intended for the bass octave only.

When studying a new piano work, he stressed certain principles of learning which may be summed up as follows: never leave a single section of a work unfinished; technique is a part of the piece itself, not a thing apart; one must musically dissect each phrase, then select workable fingerings; when each note is correctly placed, gradually put the entire piece together so that each section falls into proper relationship with the whole.

The following pages are filled with suggestions given to various students relating to the playing of certain works by classic, romantic, impressionistic and modern composers, which it is believed will be of interest to pianists and teachers generally. To understand fully each work discussed, one should have the printed score at hand.

BACH

Friedberg regarded Bach as not only one of the Great Composers but one of the "most modern" of all time and endeavored to demonstrate to his students how Bach's music transcended the so-called musical areas,— classic, romantic, impressionistic, or even contemporary. Although he demanded strict adherence to the notes of the score, he seldom laid down any strictures in the playing of grace notes, mordents, and other ornaments, believing that such embellishments were of individual taste and were intended to be played according to and at the player's grace. However, he strongly objected to the use of too much pedal and excessive rubato in the playing of Bach's music.

Taking up the "Andante" from Bach's *Partita in C minor,* Friedberg suggested to a student that by emulating the clear, pure sound of a flute, with due consideration given to the breathing or phrasing of the imagined flute-player, the cantiléna may be effected with elegant grace. For finger endurance he recommended the practice of the long A minor *Fugue*, with the six-measure subject (not from the *Well-Tempered Clavichord*).*

The Master was of the opinion that the scarcity of dynamic and tempo marks in many of Bach's works was intentional. He recalled a reference to this in a letter of Bach's to one of his sons, who had made such an inquiry, in which old J. S. B. commented that if the son could not determine the correct dynamics from the music, he had no business playing the instrument! **

"Many years ago," Friedberg recalled to a student, "I gave an All-Bach Cycle in Madrid, something quite unheard of in Spain up to that time. The morning after the first recital, a Spanish nobleman called on me at the hotel to thank me for the performance and to encourage me in playing more Bach. In discussing that composer's works the Grandeé finally remarked that one of the explanations for Bach's profundity lay in the fact that he was of the Roman Catholic faith. When I pointed out to him that Bach happened to have been a Protestant, the Grandeé answered quite indignantly: 'You are mistaken, my dear Sir, only a Catholic could have written such music!' "

MOZART

Although Friedberg insisted upon the utmost refinement of style and sparkling finger-work in the playing of Mozart, he was completely opposed to a cold, mechanical interpretation of the composer's works. He preferred that the principal

* Note: This particular fugue is difficult to identify for the reasons that there are no opus numbers in Bach's music and there are as many as *three* Bach fugues in A minor!

** Note: T. W. Edwards in Ann Arbor, Michigan, published years ago a reprint (photo-lithoprinted edition) of the *Bach-Gesellschaft* which is still available. Because it is nearest to Bach's original writing, Friedberg always required his students to study this edition.

theme in the first movement of the *Concerto in C Major, Koechel* 467, be sung with a warm tone and an ever so slight holding-back of the tempo. "A slight rubato, in good taste, is perfectly permissible in Mozart and adds much to the essence of the music," he explained. Metronomic rhythm, except in technical passages where an exact rhythm is demanded, has no place in the beautiful themes of Mozart in which there must be a slight "give and take" in the rhythm without losing the pulsation of the beat. Scale passages must never seem rushed but must sparkle with a beautiful, shimmering tone and a smooth *legato*. Each tone must sing out with clarity, yet blend into the next. A variety of tone color is essential to the playing of Mozart's music and his works offer countless oportunities for imaginative shadings.

"In my opinion," he once said, "Mozart is very consistent in the way he used certain keys (tonalities) to express definite moods, or symbols. If you analyse his music, you will find that the same tonalities are used over and over again to project similar moods, or meanings."

"Many of Mozart's works are dances of his time," he continued. "One must remember that the dress of women of noble rank was an encumbrance and that therefore dances written for and danced by 'high society' were necessarily slow in tempo. On the other hand, dances performed by people from the so-called 'lower ranks' were much faster since these people wore less and a simpler type of dress; for example, the second act of *Don Juan,* where both types of dances are played simultaneously."

Fantasia in C minor, K. 475

Because of the highly dramatic and improvisational nature of the *Fantasia* and its sudden mood contrasts, it is not easy for the student to maintain unity and coherence throughout this difficult work. The Master emphasized that the key to complete coherence in the playing of the *Fantasia* lies in providing a strong rhythmic outline. The problem is not only to establish the correct tempo relationships between the various sections, but also to co-relate these sections into the big, over-all design of the piece. Such hazards as abrupt dynamic changes, long moments of silences, insistent repetitions of a single chord, and extremely long sequences provide the pitfalls along the way which must, somehow, be fitted into the basic rhythmic pattern of the work. Unless a strict rhythmic discipline throughout is adhered to, the dramatic and tragic content of the music will not emerge.

For a deeper understanding of the intense emotional drive in the *Fantasia*, Friedberg suggested that the student should thoroughly familiarize himself with Mozart's operatic style, especially the highly dramatic music of *Don Giovanni,* with which the *Fantasia* has a close affinity. The student was then able to discover for himself that the operatic influences present in the movements of the *Fantasia* were noted in the opening and closing tragic *Adagio,* in at least two orchestrally-conceived dramatic passages, and in the *Andantino* which is pure vocal cantiléna. By comparing and unifying Mozart's operatic and instrumental styles, the student's understanding of the *Fantasia* was enriched and his playing gained the dramatic fervor and intensity that the *Fantasia,* in order to be truly eloquent and beautiful, demands.

BEETHOVEN

According to one of his students Friedberg regarded Beethoven's piano sonatas more as symphonies than as piano works; urged his pupils to examine the tonal possibilities of all the instruments of the orchestra and then strive to produce similar timbres on the piano. "One must always think in advance," he said to one of his German pupils, "and hear what the music is trying to express; if it cries and sings plaintively, or laughs and jokes, the expressive tone-color,

136

or timbre must be chosen. If one rounds the finger and presses the key with the pad of the finger (not the point), one may evoke the timbre of a brass instrument; or with a particular half-staccato in the left-hand bass notes, one is able to suggest the pizzicato of a stringed bass."

Had there been sufficient time he would have wished each of his students to orchestrate all the Beethoven sonatas. He also was of the opinion that that which Beethoven intended to express in the last sonatas was beyond the grasp of the ear; therefore, the student must be able mentally to hear with great clarity any of these last works in order to be able to play them well, to say the least.

In later years Friedberg remarked that because of his profundity, Beethoven ought to be the last composer studied. He had a great love and admiration for the *Hammerklavier Sonata, Op.* 106, and any student who studied this difficult work won his respect and gratitude. Once, in his excitement over this work, he made one of his extravagant remarks, though true for him at the moment, to the effect that the *Hammerklavier Sonata* was worth the whole of Brahms piano works! He suggested that the "Fugue" from this *Sonata* be practiced as a daily technical exercise.

Friedberg's terse definition of classical music as "the best with the smallest means" was illustrated for him in Beethoven's *Sonata Op.* 110 which, he held, offers a profundity of expression with the greatest economy of material. Emphasizing that in order to be a real musician one must have an intense love for music and one's instrument, he defined a great piece of music as "balance and symmetry of form glamorized by poetry."

"Music is made in the head," he once said, "and I feel wonderful things can be created while at rest." To a pupil who was unable to capture the mood of the beginning of the Beethoven Fourth Piano Concerto, he suggested the recollection of hearing a loved one singing from a distance, barely audible; or, that the accompanying figure of the left hand in the first theme of Saint-Saën's G minor Concerto sounds like a voice from beyond the grave, chanting "Ag-a-mem-non."

Chopin

The great teacher's own playing of Chopin inspired his pupils to a greater comprehension of that composer's music. The delicacy and warmth with which his fingers imbued the music are unforgettable. He combined a strict adherence to the score with a most wondrous imagination; it was this imagination that was the secret of his great art and teaching.

He frequently discussed with his pupils the "objective" and "subjective" performer, believing that a combination of the two, in proper balance, and with respect to the composer in question was the ultimate goal of the performer. "One must naturally be more objective in playing Bach than Chopin," he said, "but not to the point of excluding all emotion and personality from his work; for the compositions of Bach are full of deep, beautiful and noble thoughts and contain a variety of moods."

Chopin, on the other hand, allows considerably more freedom of expression, but not to the point where a performer, disregarding the printed page, distorts the rhythm with uncalled-for rubatos, or indulges in cheapening sentimentality. "Chopin is poetry," he once remarked, "and his music must be approached from a poetic and noble aesthetic. You must project your own personality through your playing in order to give a convincing, sincere performance." Naturally a thorough knowledge of the composer as a human being, the period in which he lived, and the musical style of the period, are essentials for the would-be "authentic performer."

To a pupil who brought Chopin's "Andante Spianato" to a lesson which he had carefully prepared, Friedberg insisted on the utmost delicacy, simplicity, and nobility of the melodic line. The tone must be "liquid," as he expressed it, with a beautiful legato. The melody must flow and pulsate without unwarranted rubati, and technical "frills" must not stand out as such, but must be well-integrated within the melodic line. With these suggestions to aid the pupil, the "Andante" began to emerge as poetry rather than as an inconsequential piece of "trite" music.

For practicing "staccato touch" he recommended the use of the double-shake with the Chopin "Etude in A minor," *Op. 10, No. 2,* which provides a double-note staccato.

The opening to the "Ballade in A Flat," he thought, should sound like the introduction to a story: "Once upon a time. . . ." It must be simple, delicate, and played strictly in time. In the third theme (in A flat Major, beginning at Measure 115), Friedberg preferred the arpeggio figures to come *with* the beat rather than before. The passage beginning in E flat Major, which leads back to a repetition of the second theme (this time in A flat), varies in different editions. He always repeated the first measure of this section for the reason that unless so done, the rhythm of the phrase is unbalanced.

SCHUMANN

Friedberg expressed the belief that the world has not fully comprehended Robert Schumann's music, especially his first two dozen works. He desired that his pupils play Schumann's music not only with the utmost intensity but also with a complete absence of exaggeration, or undue liberty. He often stressed the fact that in syncopated passages, in which Schumann's music abounds, one ought not to play with any rubato. Scale-like passages in Schumann he did not regard in terms of technique, but in expressivity. He once explained the entire coda of the *Allegro Appassionata, Op.* 92, as one continuous melody.

There was always an aura of spaciousness about his

teaching. The piano is an instrument through which some of mankind's greatest thoughts and beauty might emanate. The students' role he defined as "moderator between beauty and keyboard realization." Their responsibilities were presented as privileges—from the greatest talent, the greatest responsibility.

Music, for his students, began with the simplest phrase. How stunned were some to learn that they could not evoke this eloquently and symmetrically. They thought it a "comedown" to play Schubert's first "Impromptu" after Franck's *Prelude, Chorale and Fugue,* but how wrong they were! They learned that artistic skill is transferable and that the delicate nuance applied to a small work could be the essence of a large work. How much labor and intensity went into playing Schumann's "Warum." One day "Warum" was used as a test piece, each student took a turn at reading it, and all performances were anonymously criticised. How few could play "Warum" to the apex of achievement. He always brought the student back to that eloquent simple phrase; after that came every other pianistic skill.

Papillons

As one approach to the musical understanding of *Papillons,* which work seemed to elude one pupil, Friedberg conceived a little story, or scenario, for the series of twelve short, related pieces based on probable and appropriate (to the music) happenings. The fanfare-like introduction might easily be thought of as announcing the opening of a masquerade ball. Sketch No. 1 is obviously a waltz.

The ascending E flat Major arpeggio, marked *fortissimo,* which opens No. 2, might be thought of in terms of a young man's running upstairs to catch a partner who, in the following theme, appears coy,—undecided whether she will, or will not dance with him. Friedberg preferred that the last four measures of this theme in the right hand be played in the alternate version published with the original in an early edition of the work, a varied form of which Schumann himself approved.*

No. 3 suggests two business men walking down the street, discussing their stocks and bonds.

No. 4 gives the sensation of rushing and offers a repetition of the theme from sketch No. 2.

No. 5 is reminiscent of an "old folks" polonaise.

In No. 6, someone is "angry," —expressed by the general mood and explosive *sforzando* chords; in the A Major *pianissimo* section one hears strains from the dance taking place in the adjoining room.

The opening of No. 7 is meditative and oriental in mood. Perhaps one of the late-arriving guests comes masqueraded as "Fátima." The music suggests the oriental quality of an oboe in the right-hand melody with guitar-strummed chords in the left.

No. 8 is again "angry" in mood; perhaps someone is bad-tempered because he was "short-changed by a waiter."

No. 9 is rather "giggly" or "tittering," as though one had been tickeled with a fan of peacock feathers.

No. 10 opens with the left hand sounding forth with a toast frequently given at German weddings: "Hoch soll er leben!" ("Health to this man here!") The dance theme from No. 6 is repeated, key of G Major, in a more robust form. This calls to mind students with beer steins uplifted, the music gliding, of course, into a waltz.

No. 11 is a polonaise, martial in spirit. The two phrases in G Major, in marked contrast to the lively polonaise, are meditative in mood. The octaves with appogiaturas ending this section, are again remindful of chuckles caused by the ticklings of peacock feathers.

No. 12, the Finale, is the "Grossvater Tanz," played at the end of weddings. The sustained low "D," beginning in

* See the Kalmus reprint of the Clara Schumann Edition of the composer's works.

Measure 44, should be caught in the sostenuto (middle) pedal. The six repetitions of the tone "A" sound the lateness of the hour. Following a long pause there is heard the suggestion of pattering feet, scampering home to bed. At the end, the arpeggiated A Major chord might be either a sigh of regret or a yawn of relief that the ball is over.

Brahms

Concerning the works of Brahms, "the classicist with a romantic drive," as he sometimes described that composer, Friedberg pointed out a synthesis of both styles in which the outer form of the first is inseparable from the inner emotional content of the second.

After several lessons devoted to the study of the F sharp minor *Sonata,* during which a particular student seemed to be making little headway, Friedberg asked: "Do you understand the emotional content of this music?" When the student appeared uncertain in his answer his teacher then gave him the following assignment: "Write a structural analysis of this work," he said, "then write a story or emotional sequence to fit the mechanical skeleton." The execution of this unusual assignment opened new structural and emotional vistas for the particular student, providing the key that opened the door to a greater understanding and a more convincing interpretation of the *Sonata.*

The Master often spoke to his students who were studying Brahms' works, of the composer's own playing. Brahms, he said, disregarded the percussive quality of the piano in favor of moulding and kneading phrases so that the music sounded as though invoked from the instrument and not "punched" or "banged" into it, even in the large works. According to him, Brahms's playing gave an impression of great inner power, was very free, with expansive full-arm movements, by means of which he achieved a miraculous arm legato in octave passages and in the playing of large chords. This created a sense of bowing, as on a cello, and the phrases emerged with beautiful clarity as with fine speech—even in the loudest and most intense passages.

In the playing of resonant chords, instead of "banging" them out, as is characteristic of so many pianists, he suggested that the chords be formed in the air; then bring down the hands as if pressing against a cushion and imagine that one is making a crescendo before striking the keys. Brahms's "Intermezzo" *Op.* 118, *No.* 1 requires this type of chord-playing.

Friedberg maintained that in moulding and kneading phrases, drawing the music from the instrument as it were, is the only possible way to realize fully the piano music of Brahms, Beethoven, and Schubert.

DEBUSSY

The Master offered a number of helpful suggestions in the playing of the Debussy *Preludes:* "Général Lavine" is in eccentric mood; the appogiatura and chord which appear in the dance itself must not be short and brittle; instead, the appogiatura should slide up to the chord as though it were a trombone "smear" (glissando).

In "Ondine" (Mermaid), one should be able to imagine the shimmering flecks of gold in the sunlight and to capture the overall mood in the quality of tone-color used. To that end Friedberg's pedaling suggestions were helpful. In Measure 8 catch the tones "B flat" and "F" with the sostenuto pedal and hold for two measures. At the *rubato* indication catch the "D" with the sostenuto pedal and release at Measure 5 with the "D" and "A" staccato quarter notes. In Measure 20 take the sostenuto pedal for the tones "D" and "A" and hold for two measures. In the E flat section catch the chord with the sostenuto pedal and lift it in the fourth measure following, when "F" is struck. Employ the damper pedal for the half measure and resume the sostenuto at the return of the E flat chord. Also use the sostenuto pedal for the low "E flat" and hold for four full measures. The last two measures of the E flat section should be dry (no pedal). Ten measures from the end employ the sostenuto pedal to sustain the low "D's."

In "Cathedrale Engloutie" the dotted whole notes (semibreves) are to be held with the sostenuto pedal; the repeated "E," Measures 5-13, to ring clear; all chords, of course, to evoke the sound of bell timbres. Play the theme in C Major with a full and sonorous tone; when it reappears at the end, the accompanying eighth notes must imitate in a muffled tone the roar of the waves. In the final four measures take care to stress the top "G" and "E" in the left hand.

PROKOFIEFF

To a pupil who brought Prokofieff's *Sonata No. 7* prepared with an over-refined conception, Friedberg reminded him that the First Movement (with the exception of the slower secondary theme) must be played in a strict, metronomic rhythm from the opening theme until the end. "The relentless pulsation never subsides," he said, "and the over-all effect is that of a machine." The ruthless, almost brutal first theme, in contrast to the pleading, introspective second theme, provide two diverse moods which must give way to each other without destroying the continuity throughout. Thus the opening theme sets the mood of the entire movement and must be played in a decisive manner, not too fast, neither staccato nor legato, but with a kind of "half-staccato." This detached style is executed with the arm and continues throughout the movement, enhancing the legato of the contrasting second theme.

In wrongly conceiving the "Andante" (Second Movement) as a Waltz, because of its ¾ meter, the student was quickly set right by his teacher, who suggested that the pupil imagine himself taking a lethargic walk through the woods, with no destination whatever in mind. The concept of unhurried footsteps in the left hand gave the pupil the correct tempo, almost "square" in rhythm, over which a mood of pastoral contentment is projected by the melody which appears in an inner voice.

The Third Movement demands real virtuoso playing, and Friedberg counselled that dynamics must be well-planned in advance so that the player will have enough reserve power for the difficult climax at the end. Suspense and excitement are created by the incessant drive of the 7/8 beat, which must constantly go forward without sounding rushed. The continuity of the movement is maintained, he explained, by always keeping in mind the melodic line of the right hand rather than over-emphasizing the accent on the third beat in the left hand, in every other measure. The accent must be noticeable but must not interrupt the progress of the melodic line. The climax is gradually attained by means of subduing dynamics, except for shadings, so that the thundering crescendo leads dramatically into the final *forte,* and so continuing to the very end.

Excerpts from Conversations with his Students on Sundry Subjects

Pianos

To a pupil who complained about the lack of a grand piano on which to practice, Friedberg said the following: "You are not yet ready to get yourself a really good instrument. It is much better to work on an upright, preferably with a damper across the strings. In that way you will be forced to listen to your playing, inside yourself, which is a requisite for studying. Even I do not use my Steinway grand for studying, but the old upright over there. Look at this picture of Brahms—it shows him at an upright also. The same with Beethoven who, according to tradition, was offered an excellent grand but refused, and continued to work on an old upright piano."

Self-Criticism

"Do not criticize yourself while you are playing. Rather, before beginning, determine what you want to play, then sit back and watch your fingers execute your commands. Listen to what you play and only after you have finished, try to remember what you could have done better, and how you can improve it the next time."

The WHAT and WHY

"I am not interested in the WHAT; I am interested in the WHY.If you make a mistake, see if you can not find the reason why you made it. If you can, you have found your principal means of avoiding a repetition of error. It is important that you discover the cause of a mistake as quickly as possible; if you don't, you may repeat it, and the more often you repeat an error, the more your ear and memory will become used to it, and so it will be much harder to get rid of."

Practice

"When you are too tired to play, lie on the sofa and look at the score; that is almost as good as practicing. It is not the amount of time you spend practicing which should govern your work, but the quality of your practicing. Try to find ways of learning faster."

Fingering

A pupil raised the question of how to finger a certain passage to which the Master replied: "I do not like to recommend any kind of fingering until I have seen the piece played. Fingering should be recommended to suit the hand and not the hand to adapt itself to the fingering. I never attempt to recommend fingering until I have studied the hand and the playing."

"Try to play rapid passages which encompass the range of several octaves with one hand only—do not play part with one hand and part with the other. To use one hand only will give you much smoother runs, for example: 'Prelude No. XXI' from the *Well-Tempered Clavichord, Vol. I.* Apply this suggestion to the 3rd, 4th, 8th, 12th, 13th and 14th measures, but not to the 10th."

"Change the position of your hand as rarely as possible," he continued. "Very often you can arrange the fingering of a run (passage) by thinking of it as a series of chords, or hand positions. For instance, in Beethoven's 32 *Variations in C minor,*—Var. XXIX, in the first measure use the following fingering: 4-5-4; 2-4-2; 1-2-1; then move the hand to the next position: 4-5-4, etc."

Tempo

"It is important to determine the tempo you wish to use before you start playing. To begin at one tempo and then change to another while playing, unless it is so indicated by the composer, is a cardinal sin."

*   *   *

"When studying Bach, work very consciously on holding to your tempo. Even my best students have the habit of accelerating while playing a piece by Bach."

*   *   *

"Do not try to play a piece faster than you are technically able. If you play it well at a slower tempo than indicated by the metronome mark, you will still produce something of musical value. If you play faster than you are able, you will only spoil what you do know."

Playing from Memory

If a student suffered a memory lapse and "got stuck" in the middle of a piece, Friedberg would not help him to continue, but would wait to see whether or not he could find his own way back into the music. He believed that this was a part of learning and a form of self-discipline for the student.

*   *   *

When a pupil complained about the length of time consumed in the preparation of a piece and the short time it took to play it, his teacher commented: "Do you realize the many hours it takes to prepare a really good meal, and how quickly you eat it?"

Symbolism of the Triad

"The dominant is the symbol of the very essence of life. 'C' is the Father principle, 'G' the Mother principle, and the harmonic or binding note is 'E,' representing the Child, the offspring and binding element of the union."

Remembered Sayings and Ideas of Carl Friedberg

1. "Every note must be prepared."
2. "The tempo is too slow if the entire phrase cannot be sung in one breath."
3. "Silences are as important as notes."
4. "Rubato is a 'give and take.' In another place you must give back what you have taken."
5. "Bach is not square."
6. "The longest note should have the most tone."
7. "When you wish to push ahead two or three notes of equal value, start the group and play them slightly

faster; thus they remain even in their relationship to each other."

8. "Technic is the ability of the fingers to do what the mind tells them."

9. "Rhythm is the architecture of music."

10. "To start with smooth tone a chordal melody that begins on the beat, sing an upbeat (anacrusis)."

11. Friedberg remarked that Beethoven, when giving the correct tempo for a composition, said: "Allegro,—but that's just for the first four bars!" Music cannot be played with a metronome and remain art.

12. "Our first duty is to the composer."

13. He paraphrased Goethe to the effect that: "Although we must work hard, no one should smell the sweat," meaning that the actual physical strain and effort in playing a piece of music should not be apparent.

Recipe for Longevity

Carl Friedberg did not despise or bemoan his advancing years as do many aging persons; instead, he expressed the opinion that if one preserves his good health, taking care not to overindulge the appetites of the body, and occupies his mind with constructive thoughts and achievements, he will approach the advancing years serenely,—confident that they mark the pinnacle, or fruition of life. "After nature's desires no longer bend man to her will," he once said, "with advancing years the mind, or soul comes into a life of its own—objective and pristine pure—a higher state of existence many people, for one reason or another, never attain."

For the aspiring artist as well as for the man in the street he recommended: "all things in moderation." His entire philosophy of life, of which he himself was the perfect personification, is to be found in the lines of Robert Browning:

149

"Grow old along with me!
The best is yet to be,
The last of life, for which the first was made:
Our times are in His hand
Who saith, 'A whole I planned,
Youth shows but half; trust God: see all,
    nor be afraid!' "

"If my teaching you music has been sound," he said to a pupil, "you will find that many things which I have taught you will be valuable in your everyday life and in your work." He was quite right, as usual.

A TRIBUTE TO THE ARTIST

By Gerda Friedberg

Out of respect for Carl Friedberg's personality any tribute to his memory should reflect those qualities of moderation and self-containment which were so important in his nature. Nevertheless, I should like to fix for the future the fleeting fame of this significant interpreter of the beauty of music. In so doing, the picture of Friedberg as a man in all his simplicity and kindliness is no less important than that of him as an artist.

A long life brings with it the ability to relive one's experiences and at eighty a man looks back on many galaxies of friends who have gone into Eternity before him. Carl Friedberg had so many friends whose affection, belief and support enriched and ennobled his life and who affirmed as good all that he was and did. He belonged to that category of unusual beings who because of their outstanding talent can and must give much to others. He realized in his early youth that he had such a mission and fulfilled it with joy and earnest endeavor. But he always was one of the individualists; men in the mass were uncongenial to him.

He refused to be overwhelmed by difficulties and misfortune; indeed in his life as well as in his thought, he saw such as challenges to be overcome and they developed in him tensions which he as an artist could not escape. As an inner refuge from them he had only himself and his creative work, that very mission to which he was called. Music was the domain in which he could give real expression to the ideal world and through it he always sought to build a bridge between the ideal and immediate reality. Even though his responsive and sensitive nature was fully aware of all the afflictions to which mankind is subject, he held always to his lifelong faith in the ideal and believed that it could be made real through man's innate dignity.

As a man he did not fit into any conventional patterns; his way was marked out for him by the dictates of his own nature. He had the stamp of his birth and upbringing in a sound, mercantile environment but was really very little marked by it and indeed all his instincts were opposed to it. His artistic temperament, his dreaming self, transported him beyond all actual experience and revolted against all excesses of convention as hostile to his creative impulses. He was always inclined to adventure; he loved all that was bold and free and flexible. Life was for him a flux and he wished to merge himself unresistingly into its flow, restlessly and with a burning concern for all that was beautiful.

There is something of the dancer in such men so devoted to art and to love that enables them to glide over all depths, difficulties and dangers in life with graceful abandon. Loving so to mask their secret nature they cherish the belief that they can slip away before the midnight hour of unmasking.

Even in his later years his life was filled by his fantastic drive to make plans still upon a high and idealistic basis. When decisions had to be made he relied always upon his inward inspiration of the moment. Because of his profession his life was much taken up with lessons, engagements, obligations, but ever so often he had to break out of the strait jacket these imposed on him and he would throw over everything, cancel everything, run away from everybody in order to rediscover his identity in isolation. It was a compulsion he could not disobey despite the fact that he was, notwithstanding, a very serious and responsible person.

In reality he was basically shy, inclined always to run away from people and he wanted above all else to maintain this inner core of identity. One might well apply to him the Platonic saying that "to be and to exist are two different matters." Thus his life had two sides, a lighter one turned towards the world of men, a darker one, withdrawn and unfathomable. He never wanted to be tied down; he was a man of great intuition and could sense what was to come. His thinking had a sort of universal vision and he had the ability to make penetrating judgments, judgments of intuition arrived at without the need of the tortuous workings of reason or argument. His *Leitmotifs* (key words) were Symbol, Music, Art, and he could not bear to have these minutely examined or analyzed. Thus he sought always to avoid controversy and preferred to yield politely or to change the subject.

And yet he did love others and they loved him. He transferred to all with whom he came in contact the impression of great spiritual power and nervous energy. He was always surrounded by a circle of admiring women and all those around him were fortunate because he gave to them the best he had to give, and he had time for everyone. Indeed, this was the secret of his success as a teacher: to give the best and to expect the best in return. With his pupils all he said was pleasant, friendly, and without bitterness and in his shy manner he fled from the embarrassment of their gratitude.

Behind his great politeness, however, he built the wall of his reticence which acted as a "so far and no further" to those who would approach too closely and this wall was never completely broken through in his friendly relations with others. Basically he did not want to be completely understood and fled from those who all too frequently sought an unwanted intimacy. From any such situation he could disengage himself with the adroitness of a trapped wild animal.

On the podium he was always his own free self and was shielded from the world by his very selfhood. In all the hours when the spirit of music spoke to him he was merely the means of its transmission; inspired by himself, detached, enraptured, he grew beyond himself and became a true master through intense spiritual concentration. Thus he found the way to speak to others from the mysterious depths of his very soul and drew the listener into his own enchantment. This was his true world and here he lived the most blessed moments of his life. The fruit that ripened in such moments of insight was his true gift to mankind.

His patience was never exhausted in teaching and he was inexorably opposed to any haste because this was not compatible with his love of the Platonist idea beyond any performance or with the very spirit of fulfillment.

He had a sense of timelessness and even in his advanced age seemed to feel that much time still remained to him. The childlike nature of the artist, the youthfulness, never left him; life was always full of wonder and he was always in awe of its mystery.

Of artist's vanity he had nothing. He always tried to be just himself and thus to find authority without striving for it and without imposing it. The why and wherefore of his artistry, his influential power, we must allow really to remain his own secret. His memorial will be always that the way he pointed for us will live in all those who knew him. For he was an example of the true and consummate artist, a harmony of spontaneity, simplicity, and spiritual strength.

Nantucket, Massachusetts

APPENDIX I

COMPOSITIONS BY CARL FRIEDBERG
Unpublished Juvenilia

(Bingen and Frankfurt, 1883-1887?)

1. Humoresque (for piano)
2. Fugue on a Theme of Haydn
3. Böhmisches Volkslied (for string quartet)
4. Charakterstücke für das Pianoforte betitelt die vier Jahreszeiten: Frühling, Sommer, Herbst, Winter
5. Suite for String Quartet: Marsch, Andante con Variazoni, Scherzo, Zigeunertanz, Fugue
6. Variations über ein Tema von Robert Schumann in E moll (for string quartet)
7. Rhapsodie (for piano)
8. 2 Charakterstücke (for piano)
9. Fugue à 3
10. Fugue à 4 (für Orgel)
11. Scherzo (for piano)
12. Praeludium und Fugue (F moll)
13. Valse brillante (for piano)
14. Sinfonietta

PUBLISHED AND UNPUBLISHED COMPOSITIONS AND ARRANGEMENTS BY CARL FRIEDBERG

Piano Solos
15. *Stimmungen*—1)Wehmütig, 2) Ärgerlich, 3) Träumerisch, 4) Lustig, 5) Sehnsuchtsvoll, 6) Heftig erregt (Published by Breitkopf und Härtel, Leipzig, 1893)

16. Gavotte (Published by Ochler, Berlin, 1897)
17. Gavotte al "Antico"
18. Petite Etude

Songs with Piano Accompaniment
19. Ständchen, lyrics by Carmen Sylva (Published by André, 1898)
20. Todesgang, lyrics by Carmen Sylva [?] (Manuscript)
21. Über den Garten, über die Au', lyrics by Carmen Sylva [?] (Manuscript)

Reduced and arranged for publication
22. Piano-Vocal score of Humperdinck's Orchestral-Opera score of *Hänsel und Gretel* (Frankfurt)

*Seven Short Piano Pieces from the Seventeenth and
Eighteenth Centuries*
Transcribed for Violin and Piano by Carl Friedberg
with Fingering and Bowing by Fritz Kreisler
(Written in 1916-1917 at Seal Harbor, Maine. Published in
1927 by Carl Fischer, New York)
23. Andante Cantabile, Michel de Monteclair
24. Pan and Syrinx, Michel de Monteclair
25. Old French Gavotte, Author Unknown
26. Adagio in E Flat Major, Mozart
27. Rondo in D Major, Schubert
    (Recording by Mischa Elman)
28. Menuet, Haydn
29. Slavonic Lament, E. Schuett

FRIEDBERG EDITIONS OF THE BEETHOVEN
PIANOFORTE SONATAS, VOL. I and VOL. II

First edition, published by Schott, 1922
Second edition, published by Schott, 1927-1928

Plate 12
The Trio of New York, 1937. Felix Salmond, Carl Friedberg and
Daniil Karpilowsky

Plate 13

Carl Friedberg plays for his Master-Class at the Juilliard Summer-School, 1950

CARL FRIEDBERG'S SINGLE DISC
Zodiac Recording LPZ-1001 (1953)

SIDE I
SCHUMANN

I. *Kinderszenen, Op.* 15—(Scenes from Childhood)
II. Novelette, *Op.* 21, No. 4, in D Major

SIDE II
BRAHMS

I. Scherzo, *Op.* 4, in E flat minor
II. Intermezzo, *Op.* 76, No. 4, in B flat
III. Intermezzo, *Op.* 117, No. 1, in E flat
IV. An original short composition (Improvisation) by Mr. Friedberg

RECORDING BY MISCHA ELMAN OF SCHUBERT-
FRIEDBERG *Rondo in D Major*
(Victor Company)

STEINWAY DUO-ART ELECTRIC PIANO ROLLS OF
CARL FRIEDBERG'S PLAYING OF PIECES BY
CHOPIN AND LISZT, circa 1916 (?)

APPENDIX II
EXAMPLES OF CARL FRIEDBERG'S
PROGRAM BUILDING

All-Brahms Program

Played by Carl Friedberg in Bösendorfer Hall, Vienna, 1893

Sonata in F-sharp minor
Paganini Variations—Book I, Book II
Four Pieces from *Op.* 76
Four Pieces from *Op.* 118
Rhapsody in G minor
Rhapsody in E-flat Major
Waltzes

CHOPIN CENTENARY PROGRAM
By Carl Friedberg and Gerhard Tischer
Presented Widely in Europe, 1910

PART I
CHOPIN: HIS LIFE AND WORK (Short Address by Dr. Gerhard Tischer)

PART II
CHOPIN PIANO WORKS (Played by Carl Friedberg)
1. a) Ballade in G minor
   b) Scherzo in B minor

2. a) Etude in E Major *Op.* 10
   b) Valse in A minor
   c) Etude in F Major *Op.* 25
   d) Mazurka in B minor
3. a) Impromptu in F-sharp Major
   b) Polonaise in A-flat Major

CARL FRIEDBERG'S NEW YORK DEBUT RECITAL
Carnegie Hall, November 2, 1914

G minor Organ Prelude and Fugue, Bach-Liszt
Sonata in E Major Op. 109, Beethoven
Etudes Symphoniques, Schumann
Ballade in G minor Op. 118, Brahms
Intermezzo in E-flat Major Op. 117, Brahms
Rhapsody in E-flat Major Op. 119, Brahms
Ballade in G minor, Chopin
Waltz in C-sharp minor, Chopin
Etude Op. 10, No. 4, Chopin
Polonaise in F-sharp minor, Chopin

All-Beethoven Program
Played by Carl Friedberg in Aeolian Hall, New York
February 7, 1916

Sonata Op. 90
Sonata Op. 27, No. 2
Four Bagatelles
Rondo in G Major Op. 129

APPENDIX III

INCOMPLETE LIST OF CARL FRIEDBERG PUPILS

PRESENT LOCATION (WHERE KNOWN)

* Naumburg Competition Award.
† Kosciuszko Foundation Composition Prize.
** Morris Loeb Prize, Juilliard School.
‡ Leventritt Award.
* † Queen Elizabeth of Belgium Prize.
*** National Federation of Music Clubs Piano Prize.
**** Mendelssohn Bertholdi Prize (Berlin).

Ajemian, Maro (Concert-pianist, Teacher), Berkeley, Cal.

Appleton, Vera (Appleton and Field, Duo-Pianists), New York City

Bailey, Elinor Williams (Pianist, Teacher), Gainesville, Fla.

Baker, Charles (Pianist, Teacher), San Angelo, Texas

Ball, Lillian (Pianist, Teacher), Youngstown, Ohio

Beckman, Frieda Dilthey (Pianist, Teacher), Knoxville, Tenn.

Belcher, Gwendolen (Pianist, Teacher), Nashville, Tenn.

Bennett, Bob (Pianist, Teacher), Fresno, Cal.

Bobrowitz, Thelma Aronoff (Pianist, Teacher), Jamaica, N. Y.

Bock, Helen (Pianist, Teacher), Daytona Beach, Fla.

Brainard, Helen (Pianist, Teacher at Vassar College), Poughkeepsie, N. Y.

Browne, Hope E. (Pianist, Teacher), New York City

Bruch, Hans (Concert-pianist, Teacher), São Paulo, Brazil

Cafarelli, Angelo (Pianist, Teacher), Teaneck, N. J.

Callahan, Jeanne Dawson (Pianist, Teacher), New Rochelle, N.Y.

Cameron, Rosaline Briskin (Pianist, Teacher), Oak Park, Ill.

* Carlson, Jane (Concert-pianist, Faculty Juilliard School), New York City

* Carver-Burton, Catherine (Concert-pianist, Faculty Montclair State College, N.J.), Irvington, N.J.

Chagy, John (Pianist, Teacher), Newark, N.J.

† Chinn, Genevieve (Composer, Pianist), New York City

Cohn, Jacqueline (Pianist, Teacher), Métairie, La.

** Cortlandt, Jane (Concert-pianist), New York City

Criger, Eve (Pianist, Teacher), Montreal, Québec, Canada

d'Amato, Elinor (Pianist, Teacher), Orange, N.J.

Darnell, Robert (Pianist, Teacher),   ?

Dayas, Karin Elin (Concert-pianist, Faculty Cincinnati Conservatory of Music), Cincinnati, Ohio

de Roca, Emma Badia (Pianist, Teacher), Vedado Habana, Cuba

Diggs, Carol Blanton (Pianist, Teacher), Baltimore, Md.

Dornbush, Helen Wakelin (Pianist, Teacher), Biddeford Pool, Maine

Druke, Helen (Druke and Shaw, Duo-Pianists), Salt Lake City, Utah

Duncan, Ruth (Pianist, Teacher),   ?

Eising, Frida (Pianist, Teacher), New York City

Epstein, Lonny (Concert-pianist, Faculty Juilliard School), New York City

Erwin, Joseph (Organist, Teacher of Piano Dwight School for Girls), Englewood, N.Y.

Ext, Anna (Pianist, Teacher), Brooklyn, N.Y. (?)

Fehl, Margaret Kopekin (Pianist, Teacher), New York City

Feigelson, Judith Snitman (Pianist, Teacher) Montreal, Canada

Ferrante, Arthur (Ferrante and Teicher, Duo-Pianists) New York City

161

Field, Michael (Appleton and Field, Duo-Pianists), New York City

Flato, Ludwig (Pianist, Teacher), Brooklyn, N.Y.

‡, * † Frager, Malcolm (Concert-pianist), New York City

Freedgood, Maurine Stuart (Pianist, Teacher), New York City

Freeman, Joann (Concert-pianist, Teacher), Detroit, Mich.

Freudenthal, Dr. Ernst (Pianist, Conductor), Germany

Friedberg, Hans (Amateur-pianist, Business-man), Scranton, Pa.

Fromm-Michaels, Ilse (Composer, Pianist, Faculty Hamburg Conservatory), Hamburg, Germany

Gale, Richmond (Pianist, Teacher), New York City

Geiger-Kullmann, Rosy (Composer-pianist), Monterey, Cal.

Geller, Anna Levitt (Pianist, Teacher),   ?

Golz, Walter (Professor of Music Emeritus, Wilson College, Pa.), Mentone, Cal.

Gotz, Barbara Holmquest (Concert-pianist, Teacher), Ann Arbor, Mich.

Grau, Irene Rosenberg (Pianist, Teacher), Metuchen, N.J.

Haass, Hans (Concert-pianist, Teacher in Germany), (deceased)

Haimes, Phyllis Grossman (Pianist, Teacher), New York City

Hammacher, Erich (Concert-pianist, Teacher Academy of Music), Münster, Germany

Hanisch, Cläre (Pianist, Teacher), Lahr, Baden (Germany)

Hardy, Ethel Tozier (Pianist, Teacher), Peterboro, N.H.

Harvey, Christine Holzer (Pianist, Teacher), Hackettstown, N.J.

Hazam, Elizabeth Meyne (Pianist, Teacher), Glen Ridge, N.J.

Heller, Zelda Cohen (Pianist, Teacher), New York City

Hokanson, Randolph (Concert-pianist, Faculty Washington State University), Seattle, Washington

Holmes, Norma (Pianist, Teacher),   ?

Howard, Peter (Pianist, Composer, Conductor), New York City

Hubbell, Northera Barton (Pianist, Teacher Wells College), Swarthmore, Pa. (deceased)

Humble, Will (Pianist, Teacher), Joplin, Mo.

Hungerford, Bruce (Concert-pianist), Munich, Germany

Indianer, Tilly, New York City

Isaak, Donald (Pianist, Teacher), Elk Point, South Dakota

Isserlin, Niuta Schapiro (Pianist, Teacher), Forest Hills, N.Y.

* Johnson, Huddie (Concert-pianist, Teacher), (deceased)

Jonas, Dorothy Kaliff (Pianist, Teacher), New Rochelle, N.Y.

Kagen, Sergius (Composer-pianist, Faculty Juilliard School), New York City

Kamsler, Bernice (Diseuse, Faculty New School for Social Research), New York City

Kaye, Milton (Pianist, Composer), New York City

Keats, Sheila (Pianist, Teacher, Editor of *The Juilliard Review*), New York City

Keig, Betty Troeger (Pianist, Teacher), Columbus, Ohio

Keller, William (Pianist, Teacher), San Francisco, Cal.

Kohnop, Louis (Kohnop and Rubenstein, Duo-Pianists), New Orleans, La.

Kollen, John A. (Concert-pianist, Faculty University of Michigan), Ann Arbor, Mich.

Kooiker, Anthony (Pianist, Teacher, Faculty Hope College), Holland, Mich.

Korting, Marianne (Pianist, Teacher), Krefeld, Germany

Kosakoff, Reuven (Pianist, Composer, Teacher), New York City

Krehbiel, Anne (Pianist, Teacher), McPherson, Kansas

Kroman, Manuel (Pianist, Teacher), Schenectady, N.Y.

Kunsemueller, Ernst (Professor of Music, University of Kiel, Germany), (deceased)

Lang, Madeline (Pianist, Teacher),   ?

Leeb-Pichler, Laura (Pianist, Teacher), Zürich, Switzerland
Lief, Arthur (Pianist, Teacher), New York City
Liefmann, Marie (Pianist, Teacher), Frankfurt, a.M., Germany
Lightfield, Phyllis (Pianist, Teacher),   ?
Mann, Frances (Pianist, Teacher, Director Preparatory Division Juilliard School), New York City
*** Masselos, William (Concert-pianist), Princeton, N.J.
McClintock, Katherine Ellis (Pianist, Teacher), Princeton, N.J.
Meller, Mischa (Concert-pianist, Teacher),   ?
Menuhin, Yaltah (Concert-pianist, Chamber Music-player), New York City
Mergler, Daniel (Concert-pianist, Teacher), Montreal, Canada
Michna, Marienka (Concert-pianist, Teacher, Vocal Coach), New York City
Miller, Lucretia Dell (Pianist, Teacher), Bethesda, Md.
Mittler, Frank (Member First Piano Quartet), Kew Gardens, N.Y.
Möckel, Otto (Pianist, Teacher, Zürich Conservatory, Switzerland), (deceased)
Mosely, Tully (Concert-pianist, Artist-in-Residence, Texas Christian University), Fort Worth, Texas
Muehling, Sylvia (Pianist, Teacher), Kalamazoo, Mich.
Niehaus, Agnes (Pianist, Teacher), Los Angeles, Cal.
Norton, Martha Hutcheson (Pianist, Teacher), Princeton, N.J.
** Owen, Irving (Pianist, Teacher, Staff of The Metropolitan Opera), New York City
Pagels, Marta (Pianist, Teacher), Cologne, Germany
Pakter, Selma Mednikov (Pianist, Teacher), New York City
Pastor, Elizabeth (Pianist, Teacher), Ashland, Ohio
Perry, Ruth Skinner   (?)
Pew Brooks, Alfred (Dancer), New York City
Pickard, Ruth Penick (Pianist, Teacher), Indiana, Pa.

Pierce, Theodore C. (Pianist, Teacher), Leominster, Mass.
Ranck, John (Concert-pianist, Teacher), New York City
Richardson, Marjorie Wiggins (Pianist, Teacher), New Rochelle, N.Y.
Rivkin (Rifkin), Judy, New York City   (?)
Rivkin, Vivian (Concert-pianist, Teacher), New York City
Rogers, Allen (Pianist, Teacher), Brooklyn, N.Y.
Rogers, Robert J. (Assnt. Professor of Music, North Texas State University), Denton, Texas
Robertson, Jean (Pianist, Teacher), (deceased)
* Rosenblum-Kirstein, Jeanne (Concert-pianist, Teacher), Flushing, N.Y.
Rothschild, Niuta Dinces (Pianist, Teacher), New York City
Ryan, Thomas (Pianist, Teacher), San José, Cal.
Sahr, Hadassah (Pianist, Teacher), New York City
Sammons, Violanta M. (Pianist, Teacher), Westerville, Ohio
Sanina, Sophie (Pianist, Teacher), Long Beach, N.Y.
Schacter, Evelyn (Pianist, Teacher), Louisville, Ky.
Schechter, Celia, New York City
Schindler, Mary (Pianist, Teacher),   ?
**** Schulhoff, Erwin (Pianist, Teacher), Berlin, Germany
Schussheim, Israela B. (Pianist, Teacher), Providence, R.I.
Seeger, Carol (Pianist, Teacher), Buffalo, N.Y.
Selig, Gloria Zeiger (Pianist, Teacher), Kew Gardens, N.Y.
Shafer, Katheryn Rose (Pianist, Teacher), Berwyn, Ill.
Shaw, Walter (Druke and Shaw, Duo-Pianists), Salt Lake City, Utah
Silverman, Leah Binder (Pianist, Teacher), Jamaica, N.Y.
Simmons, Cecil (Concert-pianist, Faculty Idaho State College), Pocatello, Idaho
Smith, Julia (Composer, Pianist), New York City
Sollner, Elizabeth Furcron (Pianist, Teacher), Scarsdale, N.Y.
Stagg, Shirley (Pianist, Teacher), Radburn, N.J.
Steffen, Dorothy (Pianist, Teacher), Youngstown, Ohio
Steffen, Frances (Pianist, Teacher), Youngstown, Ohio

Stillman, Mrs. Leland S. (Pianist, Teacher), New York City
Stockheim, Sonja (Pianist, Teacher), New York City
Stollberg, Kathinka (Pianist, Teacher), Miami Beach, Fla.
Straus, Noel (Music Critic *New York Times,* 1935-1955), (deceased)
Stretch, Mary (Concert-pianist, Teacher), New York City
Taylor, Caroline (India), Formerly of Greensborough, N.C.
Talbott, Mary Robinson (Pianist, Teacher), Wellsville, Ohio
Talbott, Rosalie (Pianist, Music-Manager), Tulsa, Oklahoma
Targ, Paulene (Pianist, Teacher), New York City
Teicher, Louis (Ferrante and Teicher, Duo-Pianists), New York City
Thenebe, Richard (Concert-pianist, Teacher), New York City
‡ Therrien, Jeanne (Concert-pianist, New York City), (deceased)
Thomas, Helen Thomson (Composer-pianist, Teacher), Montclair, N.J.
Turner, Elizabeth (Pianist, Teacher), New York City
Van Fleet, Virginia Snyder (Pianist, Teacher), Lee's Summit, Mo.
Vessey, Norma Andrews (Pianist, Teacher), Milwaukee, Wisc.
Von Volckamar, Louise Meyer (Pianist, Teacher), New Rochelle, N.Y.
Willis, Elsie (Organist, Teacher of Piano), Big Spring, Texas
Windsor, Helen (Pianist, Teacher), New York City
Wolman, Joseph (Pianist, Teacher), New York City
Wrubel, Marshall (Faculty Geophysics Department, Indiana State University), Bloomington, Indiana
Zaslavsky, Dora (Pianist, Teacher), New York City
Zimmerman, Marilla Kohary (Pianist, Teacher), New York City

CARL FRIEDBERG FOUNDATION SCHOLARSHIP AWARDS (1950-1957)

Bashore, Sonja, Altoona, Pa.
Cantrell, Mary Anne, Urbana, Ill.
Cooper, Betty June, Great Falls, Montana
Covelli, John Thomas, Chicago, Ill.
Farmer, June, Altavista, Va.
Hungerford, Bruce, Korumburra, Australia
Kepalaite, Aldona, Kaunas, Lithuania
Lindström, Sylvi, Worcester, Mass. (Now living in Sweden)
McLean, Julianne, Wichita, Kansas
Poto, Loretta, Boston, Mass.
Scott, Vivian, Washington, D.C.
Whiteman, Lois, Great Neck, N.Y.

NOTES

Chapter One

1. Cincinnati *Times Star,* October 23, 1916.
2. *Memories of Eugenie Schumann,* (London: William Heinemann Ltd., 1927), pp. 167-168.
3. Grove's *Dictionary of Music and Musicians, Vol. IV,* (New York: The Macmillan Co., 1941), pp. 645-648.
4. *Rheinische Musikzeitung,* (Köln: December, 1913).
5. Litzmann, *Letters of Clara Schumann and Johannes Brahms, Vol. II,* (London: Edward Arnold & Co., 1927), pp. 118-119.
6. Vienna *Neue freie Presse,* November, 1892.

Chapter Two

1. Hofmeister, *Handbuch der Musikal Literatur,* 1892-1897, (Leipzig: 1900), p. 238.
2. *Ibid.*
3. *Ibid.*
4. New York *Times,* May 29, 1932.
5. John Erskine, *My Life in Music,* (New York: William Morrow and Co., 1950), p. 101.
6. Frankfurter *Zeitung,* January 15, 1896.
7. New York *Herald Tribune,* September 4, 1932.
8. *Die Musik,* (Charlottenburg: February, 1904), p. 221.

CHAPTER THREE

1. *Die Musik,* (Charlottenburg: January-March, 1905), p. 126.
2. *Ibid.,* p. 187.
3. Wiesbaden *Tagblatt,* October, 1908.
4. Krefeld *Zeitung,* April, 1907.
5. *Die Musik,* (Charlottenburg: April-June, 1910), p. 195.
6. *Rheinische Musik und Theater Zeitung XII, Jahrgang, No.* 47, (Köln: November 25, 1911).
7. *Ibid.,* "Carl Friedberg," (December, 1913).
8. From the Friedberg *Scrapbook of Clippings.*
9. *Ibid.*
10. Leipzig *Tageblatt,* December 10, 1913.

CHAPTER FOUR

1. New York *Tribune,* November 3, 1914.
2. New York *Post,* December 7, 1914.
3. Harriette Brower, *Great Pianists on Piano-playing,* "Carl Friedberg," (New York: Frederick A. Stokes Co., 1916), (Boston: Oliver Ditson Co., 1917), pp. 80-87.
4. *Musical America,* (New York: January 15, 1915).
5. *Ibid.,* July 27, 1915.
6. New York *Sun,* February 8, 1916.
7. *Musical Courier,* (New York: September, 1916).
8. *Musical Leader,* (Chicago: August, 1916).
9. Boston *Traveler,* November 27, 1916.
10. New York *American,* December 27, 1916.
11. Boston *Post,* March 24, 1917.
12. Walter Niemann, *Meister des Claviers,* (Berlin: Schuster und Loeffler, 1921), From the Chapter "Der Rheinische Kreis," pp. 155-158.
13. *The Memoirs of Carl Flesch,* (New York: The Macmillan Co., 1958), p. 321.

CHAPTER FIVE

1. New York *Sun and Globe,* December 4, 1923.
2. New York *Times,* November 24, 1933.
3. New York *Times,* January 10, 1934.
4. Worcester, Mass. *Post,* October 2, 1934.

CHAPTER SIX

1. Kansas City *Times,* June 14, 1948.
2. *Musical Times,* (London: March 1, 1883), p. 159.
3. *Musical Leader,* (Chicago: August, 1951).
4. New York *Staats-Zeitung,* April 2, 1953.
5. Toledo *Times,* January 19, 1950.
6. Toledo *Blade,* January 21, 1950.
7. New York *Herald Tribune,* February 21, 1954.
8. *Musical America,* (New York: January 15, 1954), p. 34.

INDEX

171

Op. 109, 51; *Les Adieux* Sonata *Op.* 81a, 61, 91; *Thirty-Two Variations*, 61, 147; Sonata, *Op.* 90, 62; *Op.* 27, No. 2, 62; *Bagatelles*, G Major Rondo *Op.* 129, 62; Friedberg's editions of piano sonatas, 72-73; C minor concerto, 92, 99, 114; cello sonata in A Major *Op.* 69, 92; Sonata *Op.* 31, No. 3, 107; Sonata *Op.* 110, 137; Scherzo from, 127; *Sonata in B Flat Major, Op.* 22, 133; Fugue from *Hammerklavier* Sonata *Op.* 106, 137; 136-137

Belgian Royal Family, 43

Berber, Felix, 77

Berlin, Brahms Festival, 25; State *Hochschule*, 37, 76, 77; Symphony Orchestra, 40; Beethoven Hall, 50; Philharmonic Orchestra, 52, 56n.; Opera Orchestra, 87

Berlioz, Louis Hector, 18, 83

Bernstein, Leonard, 96

Bernstorff, Count Johann von, 61

Besekirsky, Wassily, 62

Bingen-am-Rhein, 1-4

Blanchet, Emile R., 77-78, 87; music of, *Preludes*, 78; *Dix Etudes nouvelles*, 78; *Neuf Etudes de Concert*, 78

Bloch, Ernest, 9; music of, *Three Jewish Poems*, 67; *Sonata for Violin and Piano*, 86, 86n.

Bodanzky, Artur, 67, 80

Bohemian Quartet, 39, 44

Bonn, Chambermusic Festival, 40; Beethoven Hall, 40

Bori, Lucrezia, 56

Borwick, Leonard, 9

Boston Symphony Orchestra, 40, 65, 67, 82

Boult, Sir Adrian, 105

Bowling Green State University (Ohio), 106, 108

Brahms, Johannes, 6, 7, 8, 11, 12, 13, 14, 23, 24, 25, 26, 27, 30, 31, 33, 35, 39, 45, 52, 61, 66, 68, 71, 76, 80, 83, 87, 94, 95, 107, 108, 137, 145; music of, B flat (second) Concerto, vii, 7n., 8, 25, 39, 41, 52-53, 56, 67, 86, 88, 89-90, 116, 127; D minor Concerto, vii, 7n., 25; *Ubungen für das Pianoforte*, 8n.; cello *Sonata Op.* 99, 13; violin *Sonata Op.* 100, 13; *Trio in C minor Op.* 101, 13, 14; *First Symphony* (C minor) 14, 24; *Fourth Symphony* (E minor), 14, 25, 41; *Variations on a Theme of Haydn* (for two pianos) 15; G minor Piano Quartet, 15; *Tragic Overture*, 24; *Violin Concerto*, 24; *Variations on a Chorale by Haydn*, 24, 41; F sharp minor *Sonata*, 24, 142; *Paganini Variations* (Books I and II), 24, 26, 91; G minor *Rhapsody*, 24; E flat Major *Rhapsody*, 24; piano and cello *Sonata Op.* 99 in F Major, 28; piano quartet *Op.* 60 in C minor, 28; *German Requiem*, 29, 53; F minor Piano Quintet, 34, 94, 124; *Nänie* (text by Schiller), 39; *Gesang der Parzen* (Goethe), 39; D Major Symphony, 39; G Major Sonata for violin and piano, 66; *Zigeunerlieder*, 67; Intermezzo *Op.* 118, No. 1, 143; 142-143; Festivals of, (1893), 24; One Hundredth Anniversary of, (1933), 89

Brailowsky, Alexander, 81

Braunfels, Walter, 43, 46

Breitkopf und Haertel, 15n.

Brower, Harriette article on "Carl Friedberg," 57-60

Browning, Robert, 149-150

Bruch, Hans, 39

Bruch, Max, music of, G minor violin concerto, 89

Bruckner, Anton, music of, *Seventh Symphony*, 29-30

Brüll, Ignaz, 24

Buber, Martin, 90

173

174

15, 18, 21-23; other cultural pursuits, 10-11; lessons with Clara Schumann, 12-13; memories of Clara Schumann, 13-15, 19, 24, 30-31, 121; memories of Brahms, 13-15, 24-27, 30-31, 142-143; teaches while pupil, 16-17; becomes accompanist-coach, 16, 23, 32; first public performances at Hoch'sche Conservatorium, 10, 15, 18; engaged as permanent pianist for Frankfort *Museums - gesellschaft* concerts, 17; studies orchestration with Humperdinck, 18; interest in contemporary music, viii, 18, 24-26, 32, 33, 35, 43-44, 50, 91; gives first Frankfurt performance of Strauss's *Burleske*, 19; early concert tours, 19, 22, 23; Vienna debut of, 20; friendship and collaborations with Carmen Sylva, 21-22; love of improvisation, 22, 111-115, 121-122, 131; engaged as teacher at Hoch Conservatory, 23; gives first all-Brahms piano recital in Vienna, 24; interest in chamber-music playing, 27-28, 33-34, 43-44; first English tour as recitalist, 33; attends lectures at Heidelberg University, 29; interests in philosophy, medicine and psychoanalysis, 29; friendships with Hugo Wolf and Hugo Faisst, 31-32; first marriage of, 32; children of, 32; two Berlin recitals, 33; orchestral and chamber-music appearances, 33-34, 44; becomes pianist of Frankfurter Trio, 34-35, 44; offered post to head Artists Class for Pianists at Vienna Conservatory, 35; accepts post to head Artists Class for Pianists at Cologne Conservatory, 35; moves to Cologne, 35; his teaching at Cologne, 37-38, 39-41; pedagogical personality, 46-49, 74; engages Lonny Epstein as teacher-

assistant, 39; concert activity of, 39 42, 43, 44, 50, 51, 52-53; conducting of, 40-41, 53, 87, 92, 109; moves to larger house, 41; plays for Edward VII, 42-43; concert with Ysaye, 43; associations of that time, 43-44, 50-51; first Italian and Belgian tours, 44-45; Chopin centenary programs, 45-46; attains pinnacle of European career, 49, 50-53, 73-75; first Holland tour, 51; plays for Crown Prince and Princess of Germany, 51; booked for tours of Russia and U.S., 54; escapes to England at outbreak of World War I, 54-55; first U.S. concert tour under management of his sister, 55-56; Carnegie Hall debut, 55-56; tours as soloist with Boston Symphony, 65; first appearance with N.Y. Symphony, 67; with Philadelphia Orchestra, 69; other American orchestral appearances, 67, 81, 83, 86, 88, 91-92; artistic personality and attitude toward music and teaching, 56-60; divorced from first wife, 61; remains in U.S. to teach and concertize, 61-62; champions new music, 61, 77-78, 85-86, 97, 98, 120-121, 130, 143-145; gives all-Beethoven program at Aeolian Hall, 62; gives concerts for various war relief agencies, 62, 68; engaged as teacher at N.Y. Institute of Musical Art, 63, 65; second marriage, 63; two summers at Seal Harbor, Maine, 63-65; arranged violin and piano pieces for Kreisler, 64; joint recitals with Kreisler, 64, 65-67; arranges all-Brahms concert for Friends of Music, 67; chamber-music appearances, 61, 62, 92, 93-94; anti-German sentiment forces return to Europe, 68-69; short stays at Düsseldorf and Munich,

70-71; moved to Harz Mountain estate for war's duration, 72; edits Beethoven piano sonatas, 72-73; resumes concert life in Germany, 73-74; artistic stature of, 74-75; replaces Schnabel as pianist in Trio with Flesch and Becker, 75, 79; attitude toward chamber music, 76; offered post at Berlin Hochschule, 77; accepts re-appointment to N.Y. Institute of Musical Art, 77, 78; summers in Harz Mountains, 79; establishes summer home at Baden Baden, 79; tours Holland, Switzerland and England, 79; concert activity in New York of, 80, 81, 88, 89-90, 91, 95, 96; attack of rheumatic fever, 81-83; teaches from sickroom, 81-82; resumes chambermusic playing in Baden Baden, 83; Trio with Flesch and Salmond, 83, with Flesch and Piatigorsky, 85, 88-89; appointed to Juilliard Graduate School faculty, 84; social life of, 85; booked for winter European tour, 86; arranges for Lonny Epstein to take over Institute Class, 86, 87; U.S. West Coast tour, 86; first to perform Brahms B flat Concerto in San Francisco, 86; tours Germany, Austria and Belgium, 87; inaugurates first NBC radio network program of great music, 88; last European concerts before World War II, 88-89; moves to Ascona, Switzerland for summers, 90; plays at White House, 92; dismay at world events, 93; spends summer in California, 93; forms Trio of New York, 93-94; becomes U.S. citizen, 94; outstanding American pupils, 96; teaching at Juilliard, 97-103, 120-121, 128; enforced retirement from Juilliard, 104-106; Master Classes in various American cities,

106-109; contrast of 19th and 20th century attitudes toward old age, 107-108; last recital and orchestral appearances, 108-109, 115, 116; love of his pupils for their Master, 109-110, 115; concern for personal welfare of his pupils, 81-82, 127-128; condemns Century of the Common Man, 110-111; designated honorary citizen of Toledo and given key to city, 116-117; recordings, viii, 82, 117-118, 124; revisits Baden, 123; recipe for longevity, 149; last illness, 123-124; appraisal of the man and artist by his wife, 151-154

Aspects of his teaching: "singing approach" to instrumental music, 16-17, 57, 60; belief in early study of solfeggio, 122; adapted numerous methods of teaching to pupils' individual needs, 126; improvisational approach to keyboard, 100, 118; posture at the keyboard, 58; hand position, 58; making the fingers flexible, 59-60; fingering, 146-147; finger endurance, 134; accuracy in noteplaying, 126-127; legato touch, 57, 59-60, 128; conception of legato playing, 129; various kinds of staccati, 60; use of the pedals, 13, 58; phrasing, 128-129; "tone manipulation," 129-130; tone coloring, 133-134, 136-137; playing delicate passages without arm weight, 130; Liszt *Etudes* to employ entire arm, 130; technical aspects of playing, 118-122; technical studies, 121, 134, 137; scale practice, 59, 121; tempo, 147, 149; observing dynamic markings, 101; imagery in teaching, 126-127, 128; nuances, 132-133; studying a new piano work, 133; on playing from memory, 148; recipe for stage fright, 122; responsibilities in pre-

176

senting a first N.Y. recital, 131-132; a typical lesson with Friedberg, 101-102; summer-school work assignment, 131; preferences in musical editions, 126n., 134n.; lessons with Friedberg on playing music of Bach, 133-134; Mozart, 134-136; Beethoven, 136-138; Chopin, 138-139; Schumann, 139-142; Brahms, 142-143; Debussy, 143-144; Prokofieff, 144-145; comments: on pianos, 145; self-criticism, 146; the what and why, 146; practice, 146; symbolism of the triad, 148; sayings and ideas, 148-149

Friedberg, Eduard, 2, 3, 4, 5

Friedberg, Elise (née Landau), 2, 3, 5

Friedberg Family (background), 2, 3n.

Friedberg, Gerda, 63, 67, 69, 70, 72, 78, 115; appraisal of the man and artist, 151-154

Friedberg, Henrietta, 2

Friedberg, Mathilde, 2

Friedberg, Rafael, 2, 4

Friskin, James, 84

Fromm-Michaels, Ilse, 39

Furtwängler, Wilhelm, 71, 80, 82

G

Gabrilowitsch, Ossip, 50, 56, 63, 64, 79, 80, 81, 82, 83

George, Stefan, 4

Gerhardt, Elena, 32

Gershwin, George, music of, *Porgy and Bess*, 91

Giannini, Vittorio, music of, *Passacaglia*, 121

Gieseking, Walter, 73, 118

Gluck, Alma, 56

Godowsky, Leopold, 50, 58, 121

Goethe, Johann Wolfgang von, 11, 149

Goldmark, Rubin, 84, 98

Goldschmidt, Alex, music of, "Clarinet Sonata," 18

Golz, Walter, 39

Goodwin, Amina, 9

Goossens, Eugene, 92, 121

Gould, Mrs. Jay, 42

Grainger, Percy, 9, 43, 55, 79

Grieg, Edvard, 17; music of, *Concerto in A minor*, 17

Grumbacher-de Jong, Jeannette, 34

Grünberg, Louis, music of, *Emperor Jones*, 91

Gura, Eugen, 32

Grützmacher, Friedrich, Jr., 38, 43

Gürzenich Quartet, 39, 42, 44

H

Haass, Hans, 40

Hambourg, Mark, 50

Hamburg Orchestra, 52

Hammacher, Erich, 39, 46

Handel, George Frederick, 112

Hanslick, Eduard, 20, 26; author of *The Beautiful in Music*, 26

Harris, Roy, music of, *Toccata*, 121

Hausmann, Robert, 13

Haydn, Franz Joseph, 3n., music of, D Major cello Concerto, 89

Heermann, Hugo, 7, 17, 24, 28, 33

Heermann-Van Lier Quartet, 44

Hegar, Johannes, 33, 34, 77

Heine, Heinrich, 11

Heinrich, Wilhelm, 44

Hertz, Alfred, 86

Herzog, Emilie, 34

Hess, Dame Myra, vii-viii; 51, 80, 85, 105, 115

Hessen, Duke von, 87

Hess, Willy, 43

Hiller, Antonie, 9

Hiller, Ferdinand, 4, 9, 18, 37; author of, *Ubungen zum Studium der Harmonie und des Contrapuncts*, 4

Hindemith, Paul, 86, 98, 107

Hitler, Adolf, 89, 94, 122

Hoch, Dr. Joseph Paul Johann, 6
Hofmann, Josef, 23, 63, 65
Hohenzollern, Prince Carl von, and Princess Stephanie, 43
Home for Aged Musicians, 45
Hoogstraten, Willem van, 38
Horowitz, Vladimir, 86, 90, 105
Hubermann, Bronislaw, 23-24, 43
Humperdinck, Engelbert, 9, 18; music of, Hänsel und Gretel, 18; critic of Frankfurter Zeitung, on Wagner and Bruckner, 29-30
Hungerford, Bruce, 115
Hunter College Auditorium, 95
Hutcheson, Ernest, 50, 69, 81, 84, 85, 92, 104n.

I

Ibach, Rudolph, 38
Indiana University, 120
Indianer, Tilly, 120
Institute of Musical Art (New York), 63, 65, 69, 77, 78, 79, 81, 84, 84n., 85, 86, 87
International Society for Contemporary Music, 86

J

Jacobson, Sascha, 78
Joachim, Joseph, 6, 13, 17, 24, 26, 34, 37, 38
Joachim Quartet, 34, 40
Juilliard Musical Foundation, 83, 84n., 85n.; Graduate School, 83, 84, 85, 92, 96, 97, 120, 128; School, 104, 104n., 105, 106, 106n.; Summer School, 106, 108
Jung, Dr. C. G., 29, 90

K

Kagen, Sergius, 96; The Teaching of Carl Friedberg, 98-103

Kalmus, Edwin, reprint of Clara Schumann Edition of Robert Schumann's works, 141n.
Kammerer, Rafael, 118
Kant, Immanuel, 29
Karpilowsky, Daniil, 93-94
Katjwick, Paul van, 93
Kaufmann Auditorium (Y.M.H.A.), 124
Kestenberg, Professor Leo, 76, 77
Khachaturian, Aram, music of, piano concerto, 120
Kiel Philharmonic Orchestra, 46
Kiger's Operating Principles of the Larger Foundations, 85n
Kimball, Florence Page, 84
Kindler, Hans, 92
Klemperer, Otto, 9, 52, 80, 87, 93, 115
Klindworth - Scharwenka Conservatory, 34
Klinger, Max, 51
Klingler, Karl, 43
Klingler Quartet, 38, 44
Kneisel, Franz, 63, 94
Kneisel Quartet, 62
Kochanski, Paul, 84
Kogel, Gustave, 18, 24
Königsberg Orchestra, 87
Kooiker, Anthony, 96
Korngold, Erich, 46
Knorr, Iwan, 9, 18
Kopisch, 114
Kountz, Frederick J., 116
Koussevitzky, Serge, 80
Kramer, A. Walter, 61
Krehbiel, H. E., 56
Kreisler, Fritz, 23, 50, 56, 64, 65, 66, 73, 94, 104
Kreisler, Harriet, 63
Kreuger, John, 115
Kunsemüller, Dr. Ernst, 40, 46
Kunwald, Ernst, 56, 67
Kwast-Hodapp, Frieda, 73
Kwast, James, 5, 9, 34, 58
Kykunkor, (African Ballet-Opera), 91

L

Lamond, Frederic, 23
La Montaine, John, music of, *Canonic Studies*, 121
Lampe, Walther, 9
Lamson, Carl, 66
Lang, Karl, 32
Lange, Hans, 92
Lara, Adelina de, 9
League of Composers, 91
Leginska, Ethel, 81
Leipzig, Gewandhaus Orchestra, 25; Conservatory, 37; Winderstein Orchestra, 40, 41
Letz, Hans, 84
Leventritt Award, 96
Levitzki, Mischa, 79, 81
Lhévinne, Josef, 33, 50, 81
Lhévinne, Josef and Rosina, 84
Lindström, Silvi, 115
Liszt, Franz, 7, 12, 18, 23, 29, 33n., 38, 45, 49, 52, 107, 112, 113, 118; music of, E major *Polonaise*, 23; Au bord d'une source 45; Paganini-Liszt, La Campanella, 45; E Flat *Concerto*, 69, 87; F minor Etude, 103; *Mazeppa* Etude, 130
Louverse, Herr, 3, 4, 5
Löwe, Ferdinand, 52

M

MacDowell, Edward, 9
MacMillan, Sir Ernest, 92
Madrid Philharmonic Orchestra, 52
Magnus, Franz, 7
Mahler, Gustav, 20, 30, 52
Maier, Guy, 81
Mann, Thomas, 70
Mannes School, 94
Mannheim Festival, 34
Marsh, Lucy, 61
Martinu, Bohuslav, 112
Masselos, William, 96, 109-110
Mehlich, Ernst, 89

Meiningen Orchestra, 8
Mendelssohn-Bartholdy, Felix, 12, 30, 35, 37, 108, 112; music of, *Sonata in B Flat Major for Violoncello and Piano*, 18; G minor concerto, 80
Mengelberg, Willem, 80, 89, 99, 99n.
Menuhin, Yaltah, 91
Menuhin, Yehudi, 90, 91
Mero, Yolanda, 81
Messchaert, Johannes, 9, 34
Metropolitan Opera, 67, 68, 79
Michna, Marienka, 96, 107
Milhaud, Darius, 87
Mitropoulos, Dimitri, 25, 115
Mittler, Franz, 40
Möckel, Paul Otto, 40
Monteux, Pierre, 80, 82
Morena, Berta, 34
Morgenstern, (German poet), 51
Morini, Erika, 86
Moszkowski, Moritz, 80
Mottl, Felix, 30, 34
Mozart, Wolfgang Amadeus, 12, 33, 52, 76, 95, 108, 112; music of, D minor *Concerto*, 15; A Major concerto, 33; G Major violin and piano sonata, 34; C minor concerto, 41; C Major concerto, 41; *Dominum*, 53; Concerto in C Major, *Koechel* 467, 135; *Don Juan*, 135; Fantasia in C minor, K. 475, 135-136; *Don Giovanni*, 136; 134-136
Muck, Dr. Karl, 30, 40, 63, 67, 88
Müller, Valentin, 7
Munich, Brahms Festival, 44; Opera, 70
Mysz-Gmeiner, Lula, 32

N

Naret-Koning, J., 28
NBC first radio program of serious music, 88
NBC Symphony, 121

179

National Orchestral Association, 88, 123

New Friends of Music, 94

New York, Philharmonic Orchestra, 40, 56, 99; Symphony Society, 67; Philharmonic Young People's Concerts, 88; "Dollar Symphony," 88; Philharmonic-Symphony, 89, 96, 112; Federal Symphony Orchestra, 92

Ney, Elly, 38, 39, 41, 79, 80

Nibelungen, 3

Niederrheinisches Musikfest, 37

Nielson, Alice, 62

Niemann, Walter, 74, *Meister des Claviers* (excerpt from), 74, 75

Nietzsche's *The Case of Wagner,* 29

Nikisch, Artur, 25, 30, 52

Noble, Dr. Eugene, 83, 84

Nordoff, Paul, 98

Novaes, Guiomar, 81

Novak, —— von, 35

O

Ortman, Caroline, 62

P

Paderewski, Ignace Jan, 23

Paris orchestras: Colonne, Lamoureux, and Chevillard, 52

Pattison, Lee, 81

Pauer, Ernst, 29

Pfeilschmidt, Hans, 35

Pfitzner, Hans, 9, 50, 52; music of, piano concerto, 50

Philadelphia Orchestra, 69

Philipp, Isador, 121

Phillippi, Maria, 16

Piatigorsky, Gregor, 85, 89

Polk, Rudolf, 86n.

Prokofieff, Serge, 86, 87, 88, 91, 112, 144-145; music of, sonatas, 112; 3rd piano concerto 112, 120; *Sonata No. 7,* 144-145

Q

Queen Elizabeth of Belgium Prize, 96

Queen's Hall Orchestra (London), 52

R

Raabe, Dr. Peter, 89

Rachmaninoff, Sergei, 79, 87, 98, 121; music of, F Sharp Minor Concerto, 52

Raff, Joachim, 7, 9, 9n.

Rapeé, Erno, 88

Ravel, Maurice, 46, 86, 91, 120

Reading (Pa.) Symphony, 92

Rebner, Adolph, 34

Rebner Quartet, 44

Redingius, Nordewyr, 16

Reger, Max, 44, 46, 50; music of, *Quintet in C Minor Op. 64,* 44; *Quartet in D Minor Op. 113,* 44; *Variations,* 110

Reimers, Paul, 84

Reiner, Fritz, 80

Rethberg, Elizabeth, 79

Rheinberger, Joseph Gabriel von, 18

Richter, Hans, 26, 30

Risler, Eduard, 33

Rivkin, Vivian, 96

Rodgers and Hammerstein, 91

Roentgen, Engelbert, 34

Rogers, Francis, 84

Roosevelt, President and Mrs., 92

Rooy, Anton Van, 16

Rose, Leonard, 98

Rosé Quartet, 44

Rosenthal, Moritz, 23

Roth Quartet, 94

Rothschilds, 6

Royal College of Music (London), 43

Rubinstein, Anton, 3, 9, 23, 58, 63; music of, "Valse Caprice," 22, 112; Fifth Piano *Concerto,* 30

Rubinstein, Beryl, 121

180

S

St. Louis Symphony, 56
Saint-Saëns, Camille, 27, 35; music of, piano and cello *Sonata*, 28; G minor concerto, 138
Salmond, Felix, 83, 84, 85, 93-94, 95-96, 98
Salzedo, Carlos, 63
Samaroff-Stokowski Olga, 63, 69, 70, 84, 98
San Francisco Symphony, 86
Sarah Lawrence College, 104n.
Sarasate, Pablo de, 6, 24
Satie, Erik, 110
Sauer, Emil, 23; music of, piano concerto, 38
Scarlatti, Domenico, 12
Schelling, Ernest, 63, 80-81, 88
Scherchen, Herman, 87
Schiller, Friedrich von, 11
Schnabel, Artur, 33, 50, 73, 75, 85
Schnabel-Flesch-Becker Trio, 75
Schnitzer, Germaine, 81
Scholz, Dr. Bernhard, 9, 9n., 18
Schönberg, Arnold, 50, 86, 91, 93
Schön-René, Anna, 84
Schopenhauer, Arthur, 29
Schorr, Friedrich, 79
Schreker, Franz, 76, 77
Schubert, Franz, 42, 66, 143; music of, songs, 23; *Die Schöne Müllerin*, 23; D Major Rondo, 61; Moment Musicale (F minor), 66; *Sonata in B Flat Major*, 130; Wanderer Phantasie, 131; first Impromptu, 140
Schulhoff, Erwin, 40
Schuman, William, 104, 104n., 106n.
Schumann, Clara Wieck, 5, 6, 7, 7n., 9; her artistic personality, 11-12, 13, 14; celebrates Diamond Jubilee, 15; plays Robert Schumann's A minor *Concerto*, 15, 16, 19; plays Chopin F minor *Concerto*, 19; resigns teaching post, 19, 24,

25; last years, 30-31, 58, 83; on Robert Schumann's music, 121; editions of, *Czerny's Great School of Pianoforte Playing, Op.* 500, 8; Robert Schumann's works, 126n., 141n.
Schumann, Marie and Eugenie, 7
Schumann, Robert, 12, 13, 15, 23, 30, 31, 42, 52, 66, 68, 71, 76, 80, 95, 121; music of, G minor *Sonata*, 13, 121; *Papillons*, 13, 140-142; *Scenes from Childhood (Kinderszenen)*, 13, 61, 118; A minor concerto, 13, 15, 56, 67, 88, 89, 115, 116, 123, 131; *Variations* (four hands), 14-15; *Album für die Jungend Op.* 68, 15; *Dichterliebe*, 23; D minor violin and piano sonata, 34; *Etudes Symphoniques* (Symphonic Etudes), 40, 55, 91; *Kreisleriana*, 51; *Toccata*, 51; *Carnaval*, 81; *Two Romances*, 91; Intermezzo, 91; piano quintet, 124; *Allegro Appassionata, Op.* 92, 139; Warum, 140; 139-142
Schumann-Heink, Ernestine, 32
Schuricht, Carl, 52, 53
Schützendorf, Gustave, 79
Schwartz, J., 44
Schweich, Constance, 23n.
Scott, Cyril, 9; music of, *Sonata*, 121
Seiss, Isador, 38, 39
Sembrich, Marcella, 84
Serato, Arrigo, 23, 43, 56, 61
Serkin, Rudolf, 86, 95, 115, 124
Shawe, Loyal Phillips, 61
Sgambati, Giovanni, music of, *Quintet in F minor, Op.* 4, 28; *Concerto*, 33; Nocturne No. 5, 45
Shostakovitch, Dimitri, music of, *Lady Macbeth of Mzensk*, 91
Siloti, Alexander, 23, 80, 84
Sinding, Christian, music of, *Quintet in E minor*, 28
Sistermanns, Anton, 16, 23
Smith, Max, 66-67